It Feels Like the Burning Hut

It Feels Like the Burning Hut

*A Young Woman's Journey from War-Torn
Sudan to America*

By Martha Gatkuoch and
Brett Bymaster

RESOURCE *Publications* · Eugene, Oregon

IT FEELS LIKE THE BURNING HUT
A Young Woman's Journey from War-Torn Sudan to America

Resource Publications
An Imprint of Wipf and Stock Publishers
199 W. 8th Ave., Suite 3
Eugene, OR 97401
www.wipfandstock.com

ISBN 13: 978-1-61097-938-2
Manufactured in the U.S.A.

Contents

Foreword vii
Introduction xi

Part I: *Martha's Story*

1   Flight From Sudan 3
2   Uganda 8
3   Remembering Sudan 18
4   America 32
5   Thoughts 39

Part II: *The Long Roots of War*

6   Ancestors and the Sudd 45
7   White Nile and the Ugandan Martyrs 50
8   When the World Was Spoiled 57
9   Peace of the Westerners 62
10 War and Independence 67
11 The Second War 75
12 Twenty-First-Century Genocide 88
13 Cost of Technology 90
14 Peace 97

Martha's Ancestors 101
Bibliography 105

Foreword

ON A cloudy morning in July 2008, I pulled up to a nondescript gray apartment building in Campbell, California. Inside were two Sudanese refugees: two tall, dark-skinned, handsome boys. The boys and I would be heading to the world renowned Monterey Bay Aquarium. Koat Daniel Gatkuoch, age fourteen, was nearly as tall as me, and wasn't dressed for the trip but was clearly excited about going. Matthew Gatkuoch, age twelve, was dressed but not excited about going. Over the coming months my wife and I found that these were established personality traits. Matthew and I watched TV while waiting for Koat Daniel to get ready. When Koat Daniel finally emerged, we left to pick up their other two siblings. Koat Daniel answered my probing questions with short and simple answers but was otherwise quiet. Matthew said nothing in the car, being completely fixated on his handheld game. We drove about fifteen minutes to pick up their other two siblings: Paul Ruot Gatkuoch, the youngest at nine years old, and Martha Gatkuoch, the oldest at seventeen.[1]

When all four were in the car with me, their demeanor changed dramatically. They laughed and talked at earsplitting decibels in their native tongue. A strange cacophony of

---

1. All of the children have an African name, given at birth, and a Christian name, given at their baptism. Two prefer to use their Christian name, one prefers his African name, and one uses both interchangeably.

sounds filled the car as we headed to the aquarium. Many times in my life I have had the pleasure of reuniting siblings in foster care for a field trip, and I have seen their unrestrained joy at seeing each other. Usually it wears off after a few minutes, but not for this group. For the entire ninety-minute drive to Monterey, they laughed and talked in their language, only breaking for Koat Daniel to ask occasional questions.

"What's the orange flag there for?"

"It's an airport for very small airplanes."

"What's that funny plant?"

"It's an artichoke. You should try it sometime."

The love that they shared for each other radiated and filled my little car that day. It still does today.

I couldn't understand their language, but the gist of the conversation was clear. Many times I heard "Batman," "Superman," and "Spiderman." They were talking about movies. Later we learned that no one had told them that movies aren't real. Imagine if you thought Superman was real; you would spend a lot of time talking about that too! You can imagine their disappointment months later when I showed them the cables holding up Superman in a poorly edited scene from an old movie.

The aquarium was great. Paul Ruot took a lot of pictures of his reflection in the aquarium glass while trying to capture images of his favorite fish. But I wasn't there to see the fish. I was there to see the kids.

My wife, Angie, and I had just been certified as foster parents in the Unattached Refugee Minor program. All four kids, who had been in the United States for about nine months, would soon be moving to different foster homes again. Sadly, this family knew difficulty more than any human should ever have to know. Matthew and Paul Ruot would soon come to live in our home. At the time we did not know that Martha would join our home a couple of years later. We would stay close with Koat Daniel and his new foster family who lived nearby. For Matthew, Paul Ruot, and later Martha, our home would be their last stop.

Suffering is a part of being human, but there is a limit to how much a person should suffer. When that limit is exceeded, very few can recover from it. As you read Martha's story, it will become clear that she has suffered much. The fire of her soul should have been snuffed out. She should be filled with anger, resentment, and hate, but she is not. Martha's fire is lit and is burning brightly. Underneath her quiet exterior is an inspiring soul filled with hope and love, which miraculously survived despite abuse and loss through a civil war marked by genocide against her people. May we follow her example by enduring our sufferings and keeping a spark of love in our souls.

Brett Bymaster

Left to right, **Martha, Ruot Paul, Koat Daniel, and Matthew.**

Introduction

O N AN early Saturday morning a few months after Martha moved in with us, her story came out. Her brothers had already lived with us for two years, and we had spent a good deal of time with Martha who lived just a few miles away before she came to live with us. But we had not heard the story. Living out so much of our lives with these young Sudanese refugees, we often wondered what had happened. However, these stories are best not pried; they come out in their own due time.

That Saturday morning, Martha woke up at 4:00 a.m. and penned much of her story. You will read it for the first time, just as my wife and I did that morning. As we sat with Martha reading the first chapter, we cried, sharing in the deeply moving emotion of Martha and her brothers losing their family. Her story answered the questions that we'd been so interested to find out: questions of their family, their flight from Sudan, and their journey to America.

But as her story came spilling out, it created new questions for me. Martha, being a young refugee on the run, did not understand the historical and political causes of her exodus from her homeland. She experienced it, but I needed to understand it.

If part 1 of this book is the "what," then part 2 is the "why." My process of writing the second part to this book answered many of the questions that Martha's story created.

Introduction

If the reading of Martha's story generates some of the same questions for you, I hope that part 2 will answer those questions. If not, you may just want to read Martha's story a second time!

PART I

Martha's Story

1

Flight From Sudan

THE TRAGIC NIGHT

A LONG time ago I was in Sudan. I was only ten years old when my brothers and I were separated from our parents. It was midnight. My mom and my dad were sleeping in a different house than my brothers and me. I heard people walking outside with heavy shoes. I thought it was my dad because he sometimes came out to see the cows to make sure they were sleeping well. But then I realized that it couldn't be my dad because he did not have those heavy shoes. And then I started waking up my brothers. My brothers and I talked about calling our parents. But if we called them we worried they might just come and be killed. So we were afraid. After a little while, the men outside started shooting guns in every direction throughout the village. Then they started burning the house. The bad thing was, it didn't matter to the men that people were inside the house. They didn't care if they burned you inside the house. Thank God that my brothers and I got out in time.

There were groups of people outside and we started walking with them. That day it was raining so hard. My little brother Paul Ruot was about two and couldn't even walk well. It was hard for me to carry him, and even though I tried my best, we couldn't walk that fast. But then one guy whom we had known before in our village started to carry my brother. He also helped us out to find food. It was hard to get the food to eat because we were not carrying any food with us. Fortunately there were little lakes, and we went fishing there. We got some fish but did not have any bowls or pans to cook with. We just brought firewood, started a fire, put the fish onto the firewood, and added more fire on top. In that way we were able to cook our fish.

Man fishing in Sudan.

THE WALK

From Sudan we were just walking. We just started walking but didn't know where we were going. We found ourselves in a forest and just kept going until we were out of the forest. Sometimes we would find people who would walk with us for a while and help us. We thought we might see our parents again during the walk but we never did.

One place we walked through was very dry and we could not find water. I don't know how long we walked but I'm sure it was more than a month.

My brothers, Koat Daniel, about age seven, and Matthew, about age five, were walking with Paul Ruot, me, and a lot of other people.[1] We didn't know which way we were going to end up heading. Each day it seemed like we were in the same place. When we got hungry we ate fruits from the trees around us or we went fishing. Sometimes we were hungry, like when we could not catch any fish. When it came to night we were just sleeping anywhere. We didn't really care what it looked like. The next day when we got woken up we started walking. Our feet were all bloody because we didn't have any shoes on. Sometimes we were so tired that most of us were crying. I guess we thought that crying was going to help us while we were walking. We could hear the voices of the lions. We were scared. We thought they were going to come to us, but they didn't. Lucky for us, God kept them away from us.

1. In Sudan there are no birth certificates; people do not concern themselves with age. My brothers and I were assigned ages by United Nations workers when we arrived at a refugee camp.

The long road, typical of the walk Martha had to make.

THE UGANDA BORDER

It is not easy to cross the border into another people's country. Let me tell you, you don't just cross the border for fun, because I've been through it! On that day, we reached the Ugandan camp without any papers or documents to see if we could live there. They always checked people on the way to see whether or not they had papers. They put us in immigration jail for one day because they wanted to find out why we were coming to Uganda. They didn't even give us food or water to drink, and they didn't allow us to leave to get water that we knew was nearby. They often beat people to death in the jails. They just kept us inside the jail like we were their dogs. We smelled like garbage since we had walked so far without washing, but I guess they couldn't smell us because it was windy. If they could smell us they wouldn't have even come close to us. We hadn't taken a shower for more than a month. It wasn't because we were lazy, it's that there was very little water. We didn't even have enough water to drink. We were very hungry by that time. We smelled a woman cooking something that smelled very wonderful. I was wondering if she could give us some of it. But she did not. Finally they allowed us to live in the camp. We were very happy when they told us that.

We started looking for food to eat, even though we didn't know anyone to ask for help, we figured there might be someone out there who could help us. We were lucky because at that time some people who were living in the camp had corn that they gave to people who were new to the village. We got some of the dry corn and some of the fresh corn and we cooked it and ate it.

2

Uganda

REFUGEE CAMP

THE REFUGEE camp in Uganda (Kyangurati Refugee Settlement Camp) was a nice place to live. You can grow your own crops and have a free education. Later we realized it wasn't a good education, however, because the teachers didn't teach well. It wasn't the teachers' fault; it was because they didn't pay them enough, which made them unable to explain what they were teaching to the students. They spent the time in the classroom writing notes on the blackboard and expected the students to copy them; there was no explanation of what the notes meant. If you were a newcomer, it was also hard for you because they just told you to find a place to sit, without even asking you your name or greeting you. Even though the teachers weren't really teaching, some of the children were really smart; I think God just made their brains open. Later, when I came to the US, the first time I came to school I met my favorite teacher. She always came to me and asked if I was doing my work well. If I didn't understand the question, she would explain it back to me again. I was kind of hoping that those teachers in the US could go to Africa to teach those kids there.

Schoolgirl in Sudan working on the chalkboard.

The thing that I worried about most when I was in the Uganda camp was that a rebel group would attack us in the middle of the night when we were sleeping. They would just come and set your house on fire while you were sleeping. You didn't even know when they might come to you. This had happened at a camp in southern Uganda. Sometimes on the way to Kampala, they would attack people in their cars and try to steal their money. The rebels were all over the place. They would even attack you when you were collecting firewood outside the camp. This was hard for us because the only thing that we used to cook food was firewood. The first time that I heard that Uganda camp had rebels, that day I couldn't eat because I had the same problem that I had when I was in Sudan. I thought I would never hear people burning inside their houses again. I asked people how we were going to make it to the bathroom. It's not like in the US where you go to the bathroom inside of your house. The bathroom was about one hundred yards away from our house and I was afraid to walk there.

The only surviving photo taken of Martha (right) in Africa, in the Ugandan refugee camp.

One thing I really felt sorry about was that Uganda had so many homeless young kids including me. We were always begging for a dollar each day. Even when it was raining I had to stand there. Even though I was suffering. It wasn't anyone's fault; it was just that life always changes. I never knew that I would come all the way to Uganda. But who knows what bad things will come first and what good things will come after? Life gives you challenges and things change from the beginning to the end. In my beliefs, things change with time and with how you present yourself to God. If you want to live a good life you have to try to be kind to other people and not only to strive to make yourself rich. Although you have a million dollars in your house, it will finish. And whoever was poor will be rich. As they say in Africa, "Today it was my problem; tomorrow it will be your turn."

For example, in Sudan, the rich people only cared about themselves and about what a beautiful life they were living. They didn't know how other people were suffering and when someone tried to beg from them they just laughed at them. They thought that the money they had was the end of the world. I believe they forgot that everything came and went, and nothing stayed in this world.

PASTOR'S FAMILY

As I look back, some of the people I lived with in Uganda were really neat people. When we first got to the camp, we were expected to build our own house, but we didn't know how and we didn't have a mom or dad to build our house for us. I was around ten or eleven years old, with my three younger brothers from four to nine years old. Without the people helping us, we were going to have to sleep outside in the cold, even when it was raining. We would catch our death, no question. There was a pastor there who, along with his family, helped us build a house. They also helped us with so many things including growing our crops and giving us some books and pens for school. I am really grateful to them for what they did for us. Without them I wouldn't be able to go to boarding school because no one would be able to watch my brothers while I was at school.

Woman selling vegetables by the road in Sudan.

FRIENDS AND MOVIES

One of my best friends that I had in Uganda was Elizabeth. We were about the same height and we were both skinny.

When we went shopping we picked out the same colors. Some people thought we were twins but we were not. You would never see me without her; we were always together, just like pens and ink. What I liked about her was that she always was nice to me. We never got mad at each other. She also had a sweet family that took me in like their daughter. When I had to tell her I was coming to the US we were crying. We didn't know how we were going to leave each other until we said goodbye.

We liked to go shopping with friends in a small store in the village that sold makeup, clothes, dried fish, and fruits. To earn spending money, sometimes we collected mangos to sell at Lake Albert. When we decided to go to sell the mangos, we would meet in one person's house and sleep there. We would then get up at around 3:00 a. m. and walk for two hours, carrying the mangos in large bags on our heads. There were tall mountains near Lake Albert, which could take us about an hour to climb. The easy part was when you were going down the mountain, but when you came back it was really hard because you had to walk over the mountain again. It looked like you weren't even moving your feet, like you were staying in one place. It was scary because there is only one narrow road with a cliff on one side. The road has lots of people on it, and if you fall down the mountain nothing will save you. There were so many holes everywhere.

Market in Sudan.

The movies that I used to watch in the camp were not that good because we had to go to the theater, where there were a lot of people who were talking loudly and could not keep the noise down. You couldn't tell all those people to be quiet. You also couldn't get out to go to the bathroom because someone would take your seat and you would have to pay money again to get back in. But in my boarding school we had movies that the sisters bought for us which were the same ones they used to watch in the camp. We only could watch them from 7:00 p. m. to 8:00 p. m., at which time we had to go to bed. It seemed early for a bedtime but they wanted us to get a lot of sleep.

BOARDING SCHOOL

After living in the refugee camp for about three years, I got a call from a lady who was from the Catholic Church, who said they had a program that helps young girls who don't live with their parents. Every year they pick four girls to go to a Catholic boarding school called Namugongo Martyrs' Boarding School. The school was nice and quiet and was a mix of rich kids, whose moms sometimes came and visited, and the rest of us who didn't have anyone to visit us. It was tough because every day we just ate thick cornmeal paste with beans. Our breakfast in the morning was porridge without sugar. It was the same every day which was hard, but we got used to it. One day I got sick in the middle of the night. I couldn't sleep. I was just crying all night until the morning at 7:00. That night no one could help me because they were afraid to get up in the middle of the night. I kind of wanted water but I couldn't get up in my bed. I shared my bed with one of my best friends from Uganda but I knew even if I had a problem she would not be able to help me out. I couldn't understand how anyone who was sleeping in the same bed as their friend could not even wake up and help their friend out. I was thinking that it might be because I was from the village, or maybe because of boarding school racism. I wasn't sure about that. I liked boarding school too but sometimes I missed my brothers that I had left behind in the camp.

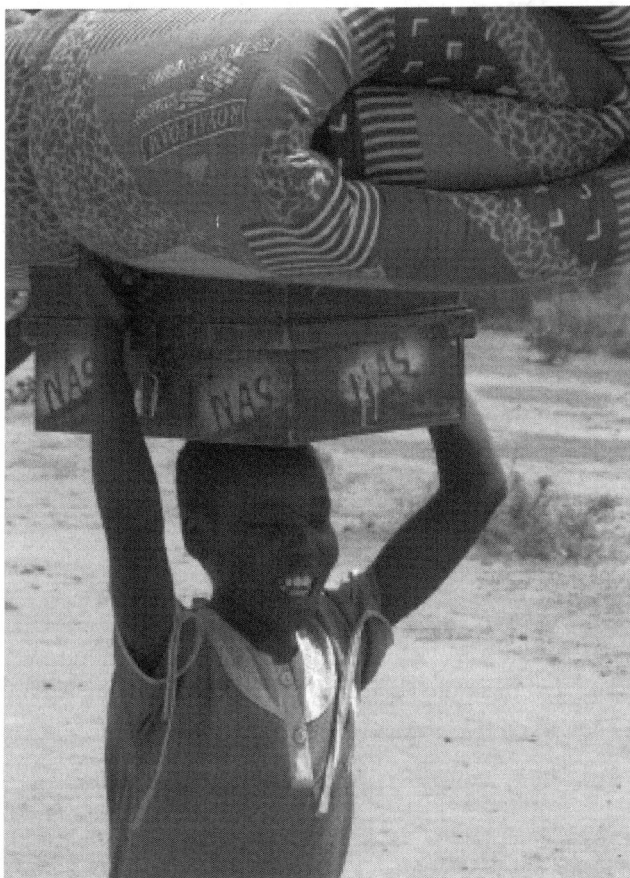

Young girl carrying her bed to boarding school.

One thing that I didn't like about boarding school is that they had tricky rules that you had to follow. If you didn't follow them, they kicked you out. Rule number one was that you couldn't go back to see your family during the school year. I was thirteen years old and my brothers were still back at the camp, a full day's drive away. Another rule was that you couldn't sneak out in the middle of the night to go to the clubs. Otherwise the parents would blame the teachers if their children were hurt. The thing I liked the most about Namugongo Martyrs' Boarding School happened on June 3. Even though it was sad, that was the day we celebrated the people who were burned to death at Namugongo. The church and boarding school were named after a group of Ugandan Christian men who were burned to death in the late nineteenth century because of their faith. Everyone came together and remembered their deaths.

Namugongo Martyrs' Shrine (Catholic Cathedral), Uganda.

3

Remembering Sudan

VILLAGE LIFE

SOMETIMES I remember the way it used to be in Sudan. During the day, the men would go out with the cows. If the men did not go with the cows, people would sometimes steal them. My little brothers would go out with the young calves, taking them away from their mothers. Then they would bring the mothers to me and I would milk them. I could balance a pail on my knee and milk the cow quickly with two hands. The women would usually work on making food while the men were out with the cows.

Sometimes, when the men were out on a hunting trip, the women would go out and tend the cows, but most of the time they stayed home and took care of everything at home.

I never learned to swim much because I was afraid of the crocodiles. I knew of several people who had been eaten by crocodiles. One man got away after a crocodile pulled him under the water and bit him on the arms, but that crocodile was always looking for him so he ended up having to move to a different village. My brothers, however, learned how to swim. They were not afraid of the crocodiles.

Arial view of a small Sudanese village.

Once I was with my parents in the village when airplanes came and bombed us. My mom called us to come out from the grass hut where we were playing and hide beside a tree. I wasn't sure if it was a great idea to hide beside the tree, but mostly when the airplane bombs came, we left the houses and ran far away from the houses so that if the bombs hit the houses we would be safe. We also let the cows out so they could run away from the bombs because we didn't want the airplanes to bomb them. Later, after we were separated from our parents, sometimes airplanes would come to where we were, and it was only my brothers and I together; my mom wasn't there with us. I remembered what my mom had told us to do when the airplanes came.

Another time I remember being in the village with my parents, when my mom was cooking for us, and my dad was working in the garden. My brothers were taking care of our cows. Everyone in my family had a little job to do. My job was to milk the cows. During the wet season the whole family was together. During the dry season, my brothers and I would take the cows to the cow camps where there was food and water. Our parents would stay in the village to tend our crops. Sometimes we sent one kid to visit our parents in the village to bring some milk to them. The journey would be a long day's walk, and they usually would return the next day. I really enjoyed that time in the cow camp.

It wasn't quite perfect, however, because the only things we could eat and drink in the cow camps were fish and milk. Some of us got sick of eating only two things without changing it. Sometimes I wished that I never went to the camps, but I had to because I was the only girl in my family, so I was the only one who could milk the cows. Before that, when I didn't know how to milk the cows, my mom used to go to the camp with my brothers to milk the cows. Some boys in the village used to milk the cows but my brothers were too young to learn. If there are no girls around, a young boy can milk the cows, but older boys and men never milk the cows. I learned when I was about seven years old. It took me about a month to know it well. When I first started, my hands were like someone put ice on them. I couldn't reach the cows; I had to sit on a little chair. Sometimes the cows got tired of me because I took a long time to finish milking and they would get up. The cows would knock me down on the floor before I could get the milk to come out since it took me so long while I was learning. That was the only job I had to do each day until I learned it. The day I knew how to milk the cows, I was so happy because my mom wouldn't have to go to the cow camp anymore and my dad wouldn't have to stay in the village by himself again without my mom. My dad only came to the cow camp once in the beginning because he had to build us a little house to stay in which took one week. When he finished it, he turned back home.

A Sudanese boy tending cattle.

Our houses in the cow camp and in the village were different. For the cow camp house, we didn't really build it well because we only lived there for about two months during the dry season. When the rains started, we went back to the village. Our house in the village took a long time to finish building. We had to build it well because we were not going to leave it quickly like the cow camp house. Most of the houses are built with trees, and some with grass. But the houses with trees are stronger than the grass houses, because when it rains the grass house can more easily fall down. When your house fell down it wasted a lot of time since you had to build it again, so you wanted to build it well the first time.

BURNING THE HOUSE

Have you ever burned down a house? I will never forget the day I burned down the cooking hut. It was the middle of the day, and it was windy. I was only about ten years old. My brothers were playing outside. My mom and my dad were in the garden. I was cooking corn in the cooking hut made of grass. I turned to get the wooden spoon when suddenly I realized the fire got into the wall. The fire went so high I thought it would touch the sky in heaven. I was so afraid! I ran outside through the door. I couldn't look back. My little brother was laughing. I guess he thought it was funny, or maybe he just didn't know anything about fire. My mom and my dad were coming from the garden running because they thought I was burning inside the house. When I saw them coming I went to hide at my friend's house, because I thought my parents were going to kill me. My mom sent my brother to bring me back home. I was sad because we lost all our food and the cooking house, but my parents still gave me a hug, even though they were mad at me. I realized that we still had family love; they knew that they could rebuild the hut back but if I was hurt they were not going to rebuild me back. I also learned that fires are all dangerous, and to be careful with them.

Cooking implements in Sudan.

LOST IN THE FOREST

There was a time when I was lost in the forest. I was collecting firewood by myself. I put all of my firewood together and tied it up. Then I started walking home. I walked for about an hour and I still didn't get home and it was getting dark. I just said to myself, "I'm probably going to be eaten by lions." I thought about climbing up in a tree because lions don't climb trees (tigers do, but lions usually don't). I thought that was a great idea, but then realized, "What about the other animals who know how to climb the tree? They will get me!" I kept going on the road back and forth. I was scared too because I heard in that forest there was a kind of cat that acted like a human. It could call you by your name and say, "I am here," and it can trick you into thinking that it is someone who knows you but it is just a cat. Then I met some people who were hunting and I knew them from the village; they brought me home. My mom was mad at me and kept saying, "Don't ever do that again!" Okay Mom, I got you. What she meant was that I couldn't go to collect firewood by myself because it can be hard to remember which way you have to go to come back home, but with two people it wouldn't be too difficult to find the road.

MY BROTHERS

Once Paul Ruot was dancing around the fire with some other little boys and he suddenly fell in. Someone quickly pulled him out but he was already burned. We did not have any medicine to put on his burns. He still has some scars from the burns to this day.

In Uganda, my brothers played soccer using tied clothes for a ball. Every day when they came back from school, they would go straight to their field that they made for their soccer friends. Their friends would come and join them to play. By the time they came to the US, I thought they were going to stop playing soccer. I didn't know that they would continue playing. I am proud of them for how good they have become. Each one of them had their favorite player. Matthew's favorite soccer players are from Brazil, their names are Robinho and Pele. Paul's best player is from Portugal and is called Cristiano Ronaldo. During the World Cup time in 2010, each of us in the family made a guess as to which country was going to take the cup. None of us got it right, except Paul who said that Spain was going to win, and it was true. He did guess it right.

To know who is funny in my family, all you need to do is meet Matthew. He always makes friends anywhere he goes and he is the kind of person who makes joy go around. He sometimes makes things up that are not true because he wants people to be laughing. One thing that he doesn't like is when someone tries to talk about Brazil soccer players by saying that they are not good players. That's when Matthew gets mad. Besides that Matthew is a very kind person who loves everyone. Another person in my family I notice who is always being honest with people is Daniel. His heart is like an open door; he always talks to people and is smiling around them.

ARAB NOMADS

One thing that I hated while I was in Sudan were the Arab nomads. They lived far away from our village, but they always came with their cows during the dry season to look for water and food. They didn't know how to grow crops but they had money to buy food from us. Every year they would come and act nice to us at first. Their time to go back to their place was usually when the rain started. Then they would return to their homes. One thing that they would do is to walk through our garden with their cows, and tromp on our crops. They would destroy all of those crops and the garden would look like we never had put anything out. But what could we say about it, since they had all of those big guns? They had already given us a warning that if we said anything they would bomb our village, plus they had already killed a lot of people that I knew in my village. One time when I heard someone start crying because the Arabs shot someone, I went to ask my mom, "Why are people crying? That person didn't die, they just shot him." At that time I didn't know the difference between dying and getting shot. My mom said that dying is when your time comes and God prepares that it is your day. I said again, "Why is it that only the women cry when someone has died?" My mom said, "Men have a stronger heart that doesn't usually cry quickly."

RIDDLES AND SLUMBER PARTIES

Riddles are really fun. I loved to do them when I was with my friends back in Sudan. On certain nights I could invite friends over to my sleeping house. The first thing we did was get one of us to go and put the beds together while the other friends were cooking our food. When we finished eating, we went directly to our beds and started asking each other riddles. First we divided ourselves into two groups and one group had to sleep on the other side of the room. It didn't matter which group went first. Here goes: "What is something that lives mostly inside the water and can change you to look like them when they don't want to eat you?" And so the other group had to choose a person to answer the question. If they didn't get the answer right, the other group had to tell them the answer. Then they could continue again. The answer to that riddle is "the crocodile," because according to superstition, when they don't want to eat you they will just take you to their house, which is deep down in the water. And usually the crocodiles that take you down there are the ones who have babies because when the mother goes to look for food those kids will watch you and if you try to escape they will cry and their mother will come back. Later when they decide to change you to look like them, they put rocks inside your knees and your elbows. Then they believe that you are one of them and you can go anywhere you want. But if you get away and go back to the village early while your brain is still human, a healer can take those rocks out of your body and you will look like a human again. If you stay with the crocodiles, however, you will eat humans, and people will be able to tell that you are not really a crocodile by looking at you. They will know that you just have the rocks in your body. The bad thing about escaping from the crocodiles is that they will never forget you, even if you move to a different country. They will just dig a big hole under the ground until it reaches your room, and then they will take you back again.

The riddles would go back and forth and until one group got twenty riddles right. Then there is a kind of silly song we would sing called "Smooth Rock."

> Smooth rock, smooth rock
> Did the trees sleep, or the trees didn't sleep
> The birds ate my ears, I'm eating the birds' ears
> Monkey ate my brain, I will eat Monkey's brain

That song was the final test. If you failed it by not remembering the words, even though you got twenty riddles right, it didn't really count to us. Most of the time when we started playing that game, it could take us until the morning. We knew it was the morning when the cock cried to tell us it was morning. Then we would fall asleep.

MEMORIES OF MY LOST FAMILY

I remember a little about my mom. She was kind of tall and a little bit fat but not that kind of fat. She had long black hair that hung down her back. Her eyes were brown like brown sugar. She had a beautiful face and she didn't use makeup because back then in the early days they didn't have makeup at all, and the people in the village didn't really care about how their faces looked. Mom always cared about other people as she cared about her kids, which is really important in life. She was a good cook. Even though it was hard to find different kinds of food, somehow she always figured out what we could eat. Mom always made sure that we ate dinner. She never let us go to bed without eating. The only thing that she didn't like for sure was when one of us went somewhere without telling her. She got mad! This was right because if we got lost she would not know where we were. She always believed that telling the truth was respectable. She didn't want us lying to her or to other people.

One day there was this tall lady who liked to fight with people in the village. She came to my mom and said, "You don't know how to fight!" My mom was just quiet. She was wondering why that lady came all that way to her house. Usually Mom didn't like to fight. But what caused her to be angry was the fact that the lady put cold water on Mom's body. It took her a moment to get up; I imagine that surprised her because she wasn't ready for a fight. But the lady was as mad as hell. She kept telling Mom, "I'm better than you at fighting." Finally she left and went back to her house. Mom just laughed at her. I bet Mom never saw someone getting so crazy before in her life.

I remember my dad; he was tall and skinny. He liked to keep his hair shaved off. His eyes were brown as milk chocolate. He always respected his family, but he also genuinely respected other people around us. He was a wonderful dad who made sure that we had enough food in the house. He often gave us the freedom to choose our own cow. He always got up in the morning and made breakfast for us, which was not great for him; most Sudanese men would never want to be seen cooking. But my dad didn't care about what other people thought. Even though they laughed at him, it didn't matter to him. We never missed going to church, even when it was raining outside.

He sometimes would go to hunt with our dog in the forest. Our dog's name meant, "Sit-by-yourself," which we chose because he was so independent. My dad and our dog never came home without meat. Our dog was known as a great runner. He ran as fast as the wind. One day, for the first time, Sit-by-yourself went out to hunt by himself without my dad. He heard the sound of a lion in the forest. He started running faster and faster to get away. Fortunately the lion wasn't close to him, which helped keep him safe. When he got home he was whimpering with fear. I felt sad about him because it looked like it was our fault that he had gone hunting by himself. My dad was mad at us and he asked us a question, "Who was supposed to watch the dog today?" Our mouths were like, "Ummmm . . ." Our eyes showed that we were scared to answer. He went out and left us in the room by ourselves. He told us to think about the answer before he came back inside the room. When he came back he got us when we were ready with a plan. Our answer was that we agreed with him, but if God chose that the lion would eat our dog that day, even though we protected him, the lion would still eat him. But God must have decided that it was not his time that day even though he went hunting by himself. That is why he survived the close encounter with the lion. My dad was happy with our answer, which helped us because if he decided we gave the wrong answer he might beat us.

We knew that dad ruled well. He made sure we did all of our chores. First, we had to clean the cows' house and make sure that we put fire inside to kill the mosquitoes because if we didn't, our cows would not be able to sleep well, which could cause them to get a disease. Another rule my dad enforced was that we had to keep our little cows separate from their mothers because if they were together, we would not be able to have milk to drink. And we learned from my dad that we would not be able to eat anything that day if we did not listen to him.

In the dry season, we usually ate two meals a day: one in the morning and one in the afternoon. During the wet season we would eat more than two meals a day because there were fish that we could eat anytime we wanted. It was also the time that we grew the corn, and most of our food that we ate was corn, as well as some fruits.

Dad had one wife and many, many cows. We were wealthier than some because we had so many cows and a garden. What could make you poor is if you were lazy and didn't tend to your garden or cows. In Sudan, our last name is from our father's first name. We have a name song that reminds us of the names of all of our relatives.

We went to church in a long building with cement block sides and open doors to keep the air moving through.

The church was a lot different than our houses, which were round thatch huts. We sang songs and listened to the priest speak about God.

Southern Sudanese round hut.

4

America

COMING TO AMERICA

THE FIRST thing we had to do in order to leave Uganda was to be interviewed by the immigration officials. It wasn't easy. Each country had different rules for the interview. For the US interview for Africans, they gave us hard questions where they tried to make us fail. That's why many Africans go to other countries instead of the US. For other countries, their rules were not like the rules for the US. For example, other countries only gave questions to big people, not to the little kids. For the US, it doesn't matter whether you are a little or big person; they will still give you the same questions as a big person. In our process, when we first started we were going to go to Denmark, but we didn't make it. We did two interviews for Denmark; the first involved taking pictures and the second involved asking the questions. In the second interview, they showed us pictures of what the country and people looked like and what the weather was like. I was wondering what made us fail when the questions weren't hard for us. That time I was kind of happy when I knew we were going to go to Denmark because we were not going to wait for a long time for our visas. But too bad for us we didn't answer those questions right. I thought that was our last chance.

I didn't know if they would call us again, because when you lose your first chance it could take a while to get it again. Sometimes, they won't ever call you again. But for us, it only took one month and it was because there was a lady, called Sarah, who tried to help us and she worked with people who gave the visas. She started helping right away when she found out that we failed to get visas for Denmark. She usually lived in the city of Kampala, but she had to come to the village for about a week to help us with our visas because she cared so much. Sarah decided she was the one who was going to give us our interview. She knew that we were not going to be able to go to the city for the interview because we would have to pay for the bus and the bus was expensive. I was happy that she was the one who would give us an interview so I would not be worried that we were going to fail. We already knew that she was not going to separate us like other people did. They put each person in different rooms to see if the answer was the same and if it was different that would make them fail. When you fail the visa test the person who interviews you is not going to tell you that you failed right away. You usually find out in about a year. It took a long time for us to go through our process. We started in 2003 and got our flight in 2007.

We almost missed it too, because I was in boarding school and I told my brothers to check for our names. The UN workers usually put the notices outside for everyone to see. They also had one in the city where my school was, but it wasn't close. I asked one of my teachers to drive me to the list. When we got there I didn't see my name outside. There were two offices. I asked in the first office but the lady there said that if my name wasn't on the list then I didn't get my visa. But I didn't give up. I went to the next office and asked again. The man inside said, "Yes," and the date was October 16, 2007. I was happy that day. I called my brothers and told them that we were going in three days. We had to get ready by that time. They took us to the hotel in Kampala for two days and then our plane came at 10:00 p.m. We didn't know anyone on the plane but some of the people were from Africa too. I was nervous in the plane and I was throwing up. The good thing was that they gave me a paper bag to throw up in; otherwise I would have just thrown up on everybody. My brothers were laughing and telling me that I was crazy. I always throw up when I go places, even in the car. But did I answer them? No, because that would make me throw up more! I just put my head down since that helps sometimes. I didn't really mind that they were laughing at me because it was not the first time for them to laugh at me and I am used to it. Later, when I would wear my glasses they would point at me, saying I look ugly with glasses. I was mad about that and never wore glasses again even though I can't see well without them. At least they stopped laughing.

LIFE IN THE US

I was about sixteen when I first came to the US, and it was cold. The place looked different to me. The first thing I did when I got out of the plane was smile and look around at all those pretty buildings. My brothers and I were worried about where we were going to live. Then they put us with people from Sierra Leone who spoke a different language. One day we had a problem with them. Things were not going well with us. They were always looking at us with angry faces that made me scared. They said, "You can't live with us anymore," so we had to leave. When they told us that, my brain crumpled up in a small ball. I couldn't figure it out, where we had to go next, when we didn't know anyone. Suddenly I realized that we had to call Catholic Charities to help us out. I called them and I had to explain the reason why we were moving out. At that time I didn't speak English well. They came and asked each of us one by one. When it came to my turn I couldn't find the words to answer the questions. I was nervous and I was just eating my hands. My mouth was closed as if they had put tape on it. Finally they decided that it was okay for us to move. But for me it was hard because we had to meet new people and follow their rules. The great thing was that I had a nice social worker who always made sure that everything was going well with us. I wondered if I had asked for help before it got really difficult, maybe they could have helped me solve the problem so that the family could have been happy with me instead of fighting and getting mad. I didn't want to leave them with angry faces. I also learned that life in this world is very difficult. You never know where you're going to end up living until you die.

FOSTER CARE

During my first year in America, I moved to different foster homes a few times. The other foster home where I had been living was nice, and the people there were helping me sometimes with what I needed. Even though we had problems going on around us, I was still happy in the foster home. Sometimes they would talk about me with their friends, and I would hear about it later, but it couldn't kill me, I would just take it easy in my heart. I knew if it was my mom she would have told me face to face if I did something that was wrong instead of "moving her mouth around," which is the African expression for "talking behind my back." People are different in my country. We called people who moved their mouth around, "scared people." They didn't have truth in their hearts; what they did was lie about other people.

There was a time when my foster mom got really mad at me because I told her that I had to go to see my brothers, who were staying in other foster homes. I didn't see the point that made her angry because we were not doing anything wrong. I just left because I needed to see my brothers even though she had said no to me. When I returned home and she was angry with me I just went to my room and cried. It kind of reminded me about my parents, how much I missed them, because sometimes when they come to my mind I will just start crying. And then I couldn't take away all of those problems that were between my foster mom and me. I finally decided to move out of that place and live with my two little brothers. They had been staying with a couple named Brett and Angie for a couple of years. I believe I made the right decision; for me, it changed a lot of things, including the fact that Brett and Angie talked some administrators into letting me get an extra year of high school at Del Mar High. Without them I couldn't go to another year of high school because I was turning nineteen. I thank them for everything that they did for me, especially Angie with her hard work. She always comes home from work and goes directly to the kitchen to make us food. When I compare her with all the foster care homes where I have been through, no one did the right thing exactly like she did, getting up early in the morning to try to make us breakfast. I felt like there was no difference between her and my mom.

Another thing that can destroy your life too is when you have the kind of friends who tell you what to do and you listen to them, when you should know better because you grew up in a place where your life was difficult. You are better off not listening to that friend. It happened to me when I was shopping with some of my friends and I told them it was time for me to go home. They started laughing and said, "You are in foster care, aren't you?" I said yes. They continued, "Then why do you care about them when they are not your parents? Don't even listen to what they say."

I said, "Is that right? If I were living with your family, would I need to listen to your parents or not? How is it different between listening to your mom and listening to someone who is not your mom?" I told them that it was not my first time to live with people who were not my parents. I grew up like that since I was in Uganda and there was no difference between the people I lived with there and my parents. They supported me and provided me with everything that I needed, paying for my school and buying me clothes. I still miss my parents, though. I sometimes feel I am not happy, like how I felt when the hut was burning.

TRACK AND FIELD

My first time running track was in my old school at Silver Creek High. It wasn't in my mind until one of my friends, Jenny, a Black American, encouraged me to do track by saying, "Come on, we are going to do it together!" Finally I said yes. I had never run competitively before.

We came to the field to run and there wasn't anyone else there. I asked her, "Where is the team that we are going to join?"

She said there is no team, we just were going to get more people tomorrow and then we can make a team. I asked her, "Is that a joke or something? You are going out of your mind!" I left her the next day to look for the coach and ask if he could allow me to join the team. He said yes, and many other people joined the team. I was happy even though it was hard to practice every day even while it was raining sometimes. But it didn't matter because if we didn't practice hard we would not be able to win the meet, and my coach wouldn't be happy with us if we lost. Even though it was hard, running track became one of my favorite activities.

People think I am a great runner. They love to watch me when I am running. But it takes me training most of a year to get my best time. Each time when we had a track meet, I would just pray that we would win the meet and that it would make my coach happy because when we would lose he would be mad and give us a hard practice. We thought that he was hard on us but he actually loved us and just wanted his team to be one of the top teams.

5

Thoughts

THE TWO THINGS I ASK FOR

THERE ARE two things in my life that I ask God for. One is to stop the fighting in Sudan. God can go into the hearts of the Sudanese and just convince them that everyone is equal instead of killing each other for no reason. That's why Sudan never really got peace. They tried to have good government leaders, like John Garang, who cared about Sudan and getting peace, and helping the women who lost their husbands in the war. He was the one Sudanese person who people believed could actually change Sudan's suffering over so many years. He tried his best to solve the problems of Sudan, though he ended up dying in 2005. Sudanese people will still remember him as their hero. The second thing that I ask God for is the ability to become a nurse so that I can be able to help people in Sudan who are sick.

MY PEOPLE

To tell the truth, many people who are from Sudan are not well educated. That is why the Arabs think that they are smarter than us. The Arabs take all the good things in southern Sudan like oil and gas that are supposed to help us. When will southern Sudan become a free country that is not controlled by Arab people? Do they have anyone left from the SPLM (Sudanese People Liberation Movement) who can stand up for Sudan and help lead a big country that doesn't really have a government? All they are doing is killing each other for nothing. Is that going to solve their problems? Do they think that fighting among themselves for many years will result in peace? They still don't realize why all their leaders that tried to bring peace ended up dead. For example, take John Garang who made it possible for a vote in 2011 to decide if southern Sudan could become independent. His main goal was to stop the fight between the North and the South. A few weeks later, after signing the peace agreement in 2005, he died in a plane crash. People predicted that they might cancel the peace agreement, but they didn't.

The great news was that the other countries helped by sending the most important people to watch the vote. For example American President Jimmy Carter was in Sudan during the vote, along with representatives from the European Union and the prime minister of Tanzania. These organizations were there to watch the election. In January of 2011, the people in the South overcame their fear and voted for independence. In fact, over 98 percent of southern Sudan voted for independence. Some people traveled from the US to South Sudan to celebrate the independence. July 9 is when they raised the new flag of South Sudan. People were thrilled to be independent! Even the people in San Jose, California, celebrated independence at a party

I attended. They were dancing and everyone was saying, "This is the moment that we have been waiting for."

CHANGE YOURSELF

In the future I want to travel to different countries and tell my story to young people who are in the same situation as me. First, I thought I was the only kid who didn't have parents. Then I realized that there are a lot of kids in the world who lose their parents. My message to all those kids around the world growing up by themselves without their mom or dad is the following: "How can you change yourself, when you know that you have had all kinds of problems?" Maybe you were a homeless person or someone who used to go to parties every day. Think and ask yourself, "Will that stop my problems?" Some people when they have a problem like that will start drinking and smoking. They think that is the right thing to do. What they don't realize is that they just destroy their lives.

One of the worst things I saw at my high school, Del Mar High School, happened in October 2010. Dr. Lovin who teaches government and economics gave us a project to do as a group of two or three. The task was to create a report on the basis of one of the book chapters. After the report was finished, each group had to present their project to the class. There were three struggling girls who were presenting that day. The topic of their report was how a bill becomes a law. During their report, they were just standing in front of the class; they did not even know how a bill becomes a law. They stood up and said, "Dr. Lovin, how does a bill become a law?" The students did not know anything about their report. Dr Lovin was mad in front of her class because the three girls didn't know what they were supposed to explain to the class. In the back of the class, the rest of the students were just talking.

High school is rough. People behave as if they were still in middle school. Things may be difficult, but you have to trust and believe in yourself, for your future. Believe it or not, as a teen in high school, people will bother you. You have to stick to your close friends and more importantly stick to yourself. Those idiots are simply human beings who have problems too, and need to make others feel bad in order to feel better about themselves. Don't give them the reaction they want—you are always in control of yourself.

MY THANKS

First, I would like to thank God for changing my life from the way it was before. Brett and Angie, thank you for your support. You are the only true family that I will spend most of my life with. I was growing up in the refugee camp in Uganda where I didn't have enough support. All I could do at that time in order for me to buy my clothes and school materials was to sell corn and sugar cane. It would take me all day waiting for people to buy them. I prayed to God, asking, "Is this how my life is going to be, only sadness?" Maybe God didn't really care about me. Then the next thing that I knew I was coming to America. God planned it for me, even though I said he didn't care about me. I was wrong, because without him I couldn't continue to pursue my dreams. He put me in a place where I had enough education and enough support.

PART II

The Long Roots of War

6

Ancestors and The Sudd

THE BYMASTER family can list our ancestors going back for six generations, which I thought was pretty good until I met Martha. Martha can recite the names of her father's ancestors going back for twelve generations, taking her family history further back than America's Declaration of Independence. Surprisingly, the South Sudanese oral tradition record of family history far exceeds my own written tradition. The name of her ancestor as far back as Martha can remember is Kakere. He was named after a dried gourd cut in two to create a bowl.

Long before Kakere, approximately one thousand years ago, African Nilotic people (associated with the Nile) started migrating into what is now South Sudan. Whereas northern Sudan is semiarid desert, southern Sudan is very moist and is covered by marshland called the Sudd. The Sudd helped isolate the South Sudanese Nilotic people from the Arab people to the north and from all other outside influence for hundreds of years. During this time a fascinating and intricate tribal lifestyle formed. The two largest tribes in the Sudan are the Dinka followed by the Nuer.[1] Martha is from the Nuer tribe.

The Sudd is infused with an endless supply of water from the world's longest river, the Nile River. The Nile runs for four thousand miles from Lake Victoria through Uganda, Sudan, Egypt, and into the Mediterranean Sea. It was the lifeblood for Kakere and his ancestors. The entire Egyptian civilization was also built along the nourishing edge of the Nile. Every September, during the hottest and driest part of the year, the Nile rose in Egypt. This happened every single year, for thousands of years, with no record of the flow ever stopping. The Egyptians marveled at this and worshipped the ceaseless flow of this river. Where could the water possibly have come from? How could it flow with such consistency in a place where the rain did not fall? The source of the Nile had been a point of incessant speculation going far back into ancient hieroglyphic records. The Egyptian god of Hapy was the deity of the yearly floods, and the pharaoh himself was thought to control the floods along with the help of Hapy. The Egyptians were aware of the Nile flowing through northern Sudan, but beyond that it was a great mystery. In the fifth century, Herodotus, known as "The Father of History," said, " . . . of the sources of the Nile no one can give any account . . . it enters Egypt from parts

1. Until July 9, 2011, the Republic of Sudan encompassed both northern Sudan, primarily made of Muslim Arabs, and southern Sudan, primarily composed of African Nilotic people. On July 9, 2011, southern Sudan seceded, and became an independent nation, with the formal name of the Republic of South Sudan. Any references to Sudan or the Sudan refer to the unified nation, while northern Sudan refers to the northern half, or currently, the Republic of Sudan. Southern Sudan refers to the southern half, or currently, the Republic of South Sudan.

beyond." Herodotus himself attempted to find the source of the Nile but was turned back at the first cataract, stating it was impossible to locate the source. The Roman Emperor Nero sent an envoy to locate the source of the Nile, but it was blocked at a great swamp, the Sudd. The famous British explorer Harry Johnston said that the source of the Nile was the "greatest geographical secret after the discovery of America."[2] Countless expeditions were launched throughout the millennia to find the source of the Nile, but every single one failed. The land of Kakere, the Sudanese Sudd, was impenetrable. The land was so inhospitable that it hid the source of the world's greatest river from the prying eyes of great explorers. The expeditions always ended at the Sudd, stymied by the heat, mosquitoes, malaria, difficult terrain, crocodiles, lions, and tribal peoples.

A section of the Nile in modern Sudan.

2. Moorehead, *White Nile*, vii.

The area that the rest of the world could not even enter was the home of Kakere. The people of South Sudan are an extraordinarily hardy people. Martha's youngest brother's name, Ruot, means, "never give up," which is an apt name from the people of southern Sudan.

In his account of the discovery of the source of the Nile, Alan Moorehead describes the Sudd:

> The Nile south of Khartoum is a complicated stream. For five hundred miles it proceeds through desert on a broad and fairly regular course, with trees and occasional low, bar hills or jebels on either bank. But at the point where the Sobat comes from the Abyssinian [Ethiopian] mountains, a short distance above the present town of Malakal, the river turns west, the air grows more humid, the banks more green, and this is the first warning of the great obstacle of the Sudd that lies ahead. There is no more formidable swamp in the world than the Sudd. The Nile loses itself in a vast sea of papyrus ferns and rotting vegetation, and in that foetid [fetid] heat there is a spawning tropical life that can hardly have altered very much since the beginning of the world; it is as primitive and as hostile to man as the Sargasso Sea. Crocodiles and hippopotamuses flop about in the muddy water, mosquitoes and other insects choke the air and the Balaeniceps Rex and other weird water-birds keep watch along the banks—except that here there are no ordinary banks, merely chance pools in the forest of apple green reeds that

stretches away in a feathery mass to the horizon.
This region is neither land nor water.[3]

It was only a matter of time until the lands of southern Sudan were opened to conquest. When they came, the conquerors found something even more formidable than the Sudd: The people of southern Sudan, the progeny of Kakere.

3. Ibid., 88; brackets mine.

7

White Nile and the Ugandan Martyrs

MARTHA RECENTLY said that her dream was to return to Uganda to attend the Martyrs' Day celebration. It is estimated that nearly a million people make a pilgrimage to Namugongo, Uganda, to celebrate these martyrs and remember their sacrifices. The story of how these Ugandan martyrs came to be is quite remarkable. Their story is intimately entwined with Martha's and indeed with all of southern Sudan.

In the early 1860s, two English explorers entered Uganda in an attempt to find the source of the Nile. John Hanning Speke and James Augustus Grant traveled through the wilds of Tanzania and up through Uganda to find the source of the Nile from the south since they were blocked from an upstream exploration through Sudan by the impenetrable Sudd swamplands. These two, the first white men in Uganda, found an extraordinary odd and fascinating people in Uganda. At the time, Uganda was divided into three distinct kingdoms: Bunyoro, Karagwa, and Buganda—Buganda being the most powerful of the three. Unlike the Sudanese Nilotic people in southern Sudan who had only local tribal organizations, these Ugandan kingdoms had a king and queen that ruled over their kingdom.

The Bugandans can trace their monarchy back to the 1300s, and to this day still adore their king, referred to as the Kabaka.

Speke and Grant first traveled through Karagwe, ruled by the king Rumanika. Rumanika was pleased to see white men for the first time, and welcomed them into his court. Speke found the customs and desires of Rumanika quite fascinating. Rumanika liked particularly rotund women, requiring them to be constantly force-fed milk by their fathers from a large gourd attached to a long straw. Their obesity was so profound that Speke endeavored to actually "engineer" Rumanika's sister-in-law's girth, finding her chest to be a whopping 4 foot 4 inches, and thigh 2 foot 7 inches in diameter! Her height was not accurately ascertainable, as she was unable to stand upright.[1] After a prolonged stay with Rumanika, Speke moved on to visit the Buganda, in hopes of locating the rumored lake that he hypothesized was the source of the Nile. He left Grant with Rumanika to recover from prolonged sickness and a bad leg.

In 1862, Speke became the first white person to enter the kingdom of Buganda. The king of Buganda, Mutesa, received Speke with great enthusiasm. Mutesa, who was fascinated by Speke, daily received him into his court. Mutesa was a brutal leader who ruled with impunity. At one point, when Speke offered a gift of a firearm, Mutesa handed the gun to a page, and instructed him to kill the first person he saw just outside the king's court. Shortly thereafter, the servant returned with full expression of glee, reporting that he gunned down a human with ease.[2] Speke was glad to

1. Speke, *Source of the Nile*, 231.
2. Ibid., 298.

have an ear with the man that would help him get to the source of the Nile, but was clearly disturbed by the constant murders committed by the king. Speke acquiesced to the strange customs of the court, which involved constant groveling and endless formalities between himself and the king. Mutesa thought that Speke and Grant's hunt for the source of the Nile was folly, and held them in his court for as long as possible. Finally in July 1862, Mutesa allowed Speke and Grant to leave, and off they went to discover the source of the Nile.

Based on reports from Mutesa, Speke had a hunch that the Nile had its source in a huge lake near Mutesa's capital. On release from Mutesa, Speke traveled to the spot, and indeed found a lake of enormous dimensions. The lake drained into a large falls and river, which Speke correctly deduced was the source of the White Nile. In honor of his queen, Speke named it Lake Victoria. In retrospect, it is incredible that it took so long to discover the source of the Nile. It is fed by Lake Victoria, the second largest freshwater lake in the world, second only in size to North America's Lake Superior. However, this was the power of the Sudd to hide the source of the Nile for thousands of years.

In 1863, just after returning to England, Speke published his journal to a wide reading audience in England and Europe. This pre-television and radio audience was rapt with fascination on exploration stories in Africa, and particularly interested in the adventure to locate the source of the Nile. Although the general public was fascinated, the intellectuals of England were not. Sir Richard Francis Burton, another famous explorer of Africa, launched an attack on Speke's work, calling his competency and honesty into question. Sir David Livingstone himself weighed in on the discovery, stating that there was no question that the source of the Nile was south of the equator, and certainly far south of what Speke claimed. On September 15, 1864, the day before defending his book in public debate against Burton, Speke tripped while crossing a fence, fell on his discharging gun, and was killed. The poor man survived years of danger in the African bush to make the greatest geographical discovery of the nineteenth century only to accidentally kill himself while being disgraced by a wrongfully critical audience.

By the mid 1870s missionaries fascinated by Speke's writing were packing up to head to Uganda. Alexander Mackay, a Scottish Protestant, and Siméon Lourdel, a French Catholic, became Uganda's competing missionaries in Mutesa's court. Mutesa, now twenty years older than when Speke saw him, was aging quickly due to his gluttonous indulgences. He had been proselytized by the Arab slavers who had already been instructing him in Islam for many years. The ways of Islam were amicable to him, with its allowances for polygamy and slaves, but he was never fully recognized as a Muslim since he refused to be circumcised. But Mutesa felt he needed the Christian missionaries in order to get supplies and weapons from Europe, and to equip himself for the colonization that he knew could follow.

The Anglican Mackay had a deep dislike of the Catholics, and immediately upon Lourdel's arrival he disparaged the Catholics in Mutesa's court. Mutesa very much enjoyed the debate of the two missionaries who disagreed so much over their beliefs, which were practically the same.

Mutesa enjoyed summoning the two and provoking an argument. Although Mutesa never himself picked sides, he did allow his court and his people to convert to the religion of their choosing.

In spite of their non-ecumenical debate, Lourdel and Mackay made amazing progress in proselytizing Ugandans, and even made halting progress on proselytizing Mutesa. In 1879, Mutesa requested to be baptized by Lourdel, but Lourdel declined due to Mutesa's polygamy. Mutesa at one point sent three Bugandans as envoys to England to ask for the hand of the Queen of England. In his delusional grandeur, Mutesa thought the queen would be a wife of standing equal only to himself.[3] Lourdel was winning over converts with his lingual skills, as he began to translate Lugandan (the local dialect), and to create a written dictionary of the language. To generate future converts, Lourdel ransomed slaves, and by 1882 had rescued forty children from slavery and raised them in an orphanage. Converts continued to build, even when Lourdel left the area for a few years in the early 1880s.[4]

The faith of these two men must have been remarkable. In the course of just a few years, they were able to convert a large number of Bugandans to Christianity.

In 1884, two apparently unrelated events occurred that changed everything for these two missionaries' converts. First, a new route was opened to Buganda using an eastern approach around Lake Victoria from Zanzibar, cutting in half the time required to travel to Buganda. Second, Mutesa died. Both of these seemed to be good news for the

3. Moorehead, *White Nile*, 320.
4. Shorter, "Lourdel Siméon, 1853–1890."

missionaries, since Mutesa's son and successor, Mwanga, had been sympathetic to the Christians while Mutesa was on the throne.

Soon after Mwanga took the throne, a new missionary decided to take the new direct route to Uganda from the East. Unfortunately, there was a longstanding Bugandan legend that a foreigner coming from the east would defeat the country. When Mwanga heard of this, he sent an order to kill the missionary, which was carried out. After this point, Mwanga became an erratic, unpredictable, and brutal king. He was intensely afraid of invasion by Europeans, or being overrun by the Arab Mahdi's movement that was building steam in Sudan; neither fear was unwarranted. Mwanga decided that the existence of Christianity within his court was a liability, as it provided easy access to the foreigners.

The breaking point for Mwanga came when he solicited some young Christians for homosexual practices. The young followers refused, and the king flew into an uncontrolled rage. He assembled a large number of pages in his court, and asked all of the Christians to step forward. Mwanga demanded that they renounce their faith and revert to their traditional ways. The pages refused and were led out and burned alive en mass. Executioners were deeply moved by the attitudes of the Christians as they burned. When the fires were lit, no screaming or crying was heard. Only prayers to God were heard as they burned to death.[5] Over the course of 1885 to 1887, the massacre continued. Amazingly, however, the Christians, both Protestant and

5. Uganda Martyrs Shrine, http://www.ugandamartyrsshrine.org
.ug/details.php?id=8.

Catholic, continued to meet secretly with Mackay and Lourdel throughout the holocaust.

The faith of these martyrs was truly astounding. Uganda today is 85 percent Christian, a legacy that is largely based on the faith of these martyrs. Martha's boarding school, located in Namugongo, is in the exact location in which the martyrs were incinerated. In 1964, Pope Paul VI canonized twenty-two of the martyrs at the Basilica Church of the Uganda Martyrs in Namugongo. On June 3, the whole country of Uganda along with pilgrims from all over Africa and the world stop to celebrate Martyrs' Day, a national holiday. Namugongo and the surrounding city of Kampala swell as nearly a million people celebrate this holiday.

The legacy of the martyrs has made a deep impact on Martha and her faith. She spent several years at the boarding school at Namugongo, attending the Basilica of the Martyrs. These martyrs represent an example of how to live a strong Christian faith even in the light of intense suffering. The peace and joy of the martyrs while their executioners were lighting the fire are a testament to the power of God in terrible situations. I have the joy of watching that power in Martha. Through all of her sufferings and struggles, the power of Jesus shines in her life.

8

When the World was Spoiled

WHILE ISOLATED for a thousand years from outside pressures by the Sudd, the Nuer developed a lifestyle revolving around their most precious possession: cattle. Everything in Nuer life revolved around the cattle. A wealthy family could own more than one hundred fifty cattle. Cattle were not primarily used as meat; rather, they were used for milk, blood, and currency. A very important aspect of Nuer life was the dowry. When a marriage occurred, the father of the groom paid a dowry to the bride in cattle. Often a very large number of cattle changed hands, perhaps up to fifty cattle for wealthy families, a sum that is worth tens of thousands of dollars. If the marriage ended in a divorce, or in infertility, the cows had to be returned. The people had no written language to keep track of the cattle, but knew each individual cow by name and its origin in case it had to be returned.

Most South Sudanese people describe their homeland as something approaching paradise. The wet climate is well suited to raise cattle and simple crops. The extended period of isolation allowed a well-balanced, family-oriented society to develop and thrive.

The beautiful land of southern Sudan.

Before Kakere was born, northern Sudan was composed of three Christian kingdoms: Nubia, Muqurra, and Alwa, collectively referred to as the Nubian kingdoms. These kingdoms began to form around the sixth century AD. According to the tradition of the kingdoms, a missionary from Byzantine, Empress Theodora, came to the region to preach the gospel in 540 AD. The three Nubian kingdoms accepted Christ, and placed themselves under the authority of the Coptic patriarch Alexandria.[1] These Coptic Christians had a strong faith that had endured for over a thousand years, but by the time Kakere came along, things had changed.

1. Metz, *Sudan*, 8.

After Mohammed's death in 632 AD, Islam started spreading throughout the Arab region and into northern Africa. The Nubian Christians were not interested in converting and instead struck treaties with the powerful Arab armies. This lasted for six hundred years, but eventually they started to falter under Arab pressure. The Nubians still refused to convert, and were eventually conquered by Arabs. The Nubians still exist today as a distinct peoples group; however, they now practice Islam.

An uninterrupted string of perhaps fifty Nuer marriages had preceded Kakere, and undoubtedly he thought another fifty were to come. However, the seeds of war that would interrupt his unbroken lineage were being planted even at that time, which would come to fruition twelve generations later. That war would finally wrench his great-(x9)-granddaughter from her homeland. It would have been impossible for Kakere to imagine the sequence of events that were taking place one thousand miles to the north that would eventually have such a dramatic effect on his family. Kakere had never known any outside influence. As far as he knew, the whole world was composed of the Dinka, Nuer, and a myriad of smaller tribes in the region. But the wheels of fate had already begun spinning, and by the time Kakere was born, the war two hundred years in the future was already a certainty, as the technology to penetrate the Sudd was inevitable.

By the time Kakere was born in the 1700s, Nubia was gone. Northern Sudan had become Muslim, and was ruled by the kingdom of Funj. Kakere's son Keer and his grandson Jiohk lived during a time of significant change in northern Sudan, changes which for the first time would bring outside influence into their lives. The Turkish Ottoman leader, Muhammad Ali Pasha, defeated the Funj kingdom in 1821, and ruled through 1885. Egyptian armies were filled with slaves who were forced to fight for the Egyptians. The regional supply of slaves in northern Sudan proved insufficient to fill the ranks of the armies, and for the first time in almost one thousand years, foreigners broke the impenetrable Sudd. Jiohk's idyllically isolated people were invaded by slave raiders. The Nilotic people referred to this as "the time when the world was spoiled."[2]

This led to the slow demise of their centuries-old way of life. As would future invaders, the slave raiders plundered the land and the people, giving nothing in return. The slave trade was an evil conspiracy against a defenseless people. It left a shameful mark on the western "advanced" society—advanced only for the wealthy at the expense of the Africans. Moorehead describes the evil scourge of slavery:

> The Khartoum slavers would fall upon some neighboring village in the night, firing the huts just before dawn and shooting into the flames. It was the women that the slavers chiefly wanted, and these were secured by placing a heavy forked pole known as a sheba on their shoulders. The head was locked in by a crossbar, the hands were tied to the pole in the front, and the children were bound to their mothers by a chain passed round their necks. Everything the village contained would be looted—cattle, ivory, grain, even the crude jewelry that was cut off the dead victims— and the whole cavalcade would be marched back

2. F. Deng, *Africans of Two Worlds*, 130–42.

to the river to await shipment to Khartoum . . .
From 50 to 100 dollars (approximately 10 to 20
pounds) would be paid for a pretty young con-
cubine, who would be obliged to undress and
submit to the usual handling before she was
purchased . . . It was no uncommon thing to see
a slave slashed with a knife. Salt was sometimes
rubbed into the wound, and other worse mutila-
tions were inflicted as well.[3]

The slave raiding continued unabated throughout the
time of Jiohk, his son Quane, and his grandson Jahl. They
probably lived in fear of returning home from a hunting trip
to find their family gone. During the time of Martha's ancestor Jahl, the slave trade was officially outlawed in Egypt
under pressure from the abolitionist England. However,
this policy was not enforced. The impact of the slave trade
had become so extreme that whole communities and towns
outside Khartoum were abandoned. The remote villages far
from the Nile were protected by lack of access, but as time
went on, the slavers became greedier and eventually much
of Sudan was ravaged by the slave trade.

3. Moorehead, *White Nile*, 85, 309–10.

9

Peace of the Westerners

DURING THE life of Jahl's son Kucck, a famous Englishman named Charles Gordon was assigned to the job of officially ending slavery in Sudan. England had been staunchly abolitionist since the late 1700s. By 1833 England had abolished slavery in all her colonies, and started actively trying to suppress slavery worldwide. She concentrated much of her effort on Sudan. In 1878, one of Gordon's commanders, Romolo Gessi, defeated a major slaver in southern Sudan and freed ten thousand slaves in one fell swoop.[1]

However, the local traditions of slaving were difficult to change. In fact, slavery exists to this day in Sudan.

During the lives of Martha's ancestors Kucck and Gong, a fanatical Muslim movement started taking hold throughout Sudan. This was the first of the unified nationalistic Sudanese movements. The breadth and scope of this movement was such that it is quite possible that Kucck and Gong were aware that things were beginning to change. A radical Muslim, Mohammed Ahmed Ibn el-Sayyid Abdullah, declared himself the Mahdi—a messianic redeemer of the

1. Moorehead, *White Nile*, 207.

Muslims. The Mahdi was a passionate, charismatic, and brutal leader. He was said to have smiled at everything: eating, sleeping, and killing.[2] His ambitions were impressive. He harbored a deep hatred of Egypt, and England by proxy, and planned to expel both from the Sudan. He then planned to defeat Egypt, cross the Suez Canal, and defeat Jerusalem, at which time Jesus would descend from heaven to meet him.[3] Islam would then conquer the whole world. He was ambitious indeed!

Gordon's anti-slave campaign had turned into a colonistic governorship in Khartoum, as he'd lost much of his abolitionist ideals. The Mahdi then trapped him there by putting the city to siege for six months. General Gordon was one of the most popular figures in England at the time. Although England was uninterested in truly colonizing Sudan, popular support of Gordon necessitated a rescue mission to extract him from the Mahdi's entrapment. However, the rescue crew moved slowly through the desert from Egypt to Khartoum. On January 28, 1885, the rescue mission arrived in Khartoum two days late, only to find Gordon's head hanging from a tree and the Mahdi in control of Sudan.

The Mahdi's messianic campaign ended suddenly when he died only six months later of typhus. He had appointed successors, but his regime did not last. However, the radical Muslim movement as a whole continued. Under English rule, it was forcefully suppressed but not snuffed out. After a fifty-year hiatus, it returned.

2. Ibid., 229.
3. Ibid., 231.

In 1899, England established joint control over the Sudan along with Egypt. The English ended slavery and again tried to isolate the South from outside influence. They stopped Northerners from crossing into South Sudan, allowing the southern Sudanese to proceed in their tribal customs. The British developed and educated the North while paying little attention to the South. They did try to monetize the South, but ultimately failed to get the Nilotic people to move away from their cow-based economy. Instead people integrated money into their traditional culture. If one suspected a drought or war was coming, he sold his cattle, held the money, and then bought a new herd after things improved. In this way, British money reinforced tribal ways. But in other ways it weakened their culture by encouraging young men to go away to Khartoum as immigrant construction workers in order to buy trinkets to impress women.[4]

This was probably a fairly good time for Martha's ancestors Gong and her great-great grandfather, Luak. They were likely relatively free from worry of slave traders as life returned to the normal worries of cows and crops.

For the most part, the English were benevolent rulers. There was no question that someone would colonize Sudan and the Muslim Mahdist that preceded them and the Muslim government that followed them would both be worse for the Southerners. As a third party in the South, the British were able to bring peace and governmental organization. No doubt there was some exploitation by them, but they did bring peace and stability to Sudan.

4. Hutchinson, *Nuer Dilemmas*, 26.

Henry Jackson was a veteran administrator in the British-Egyptian Condominium in Sudan in the early 1900s. His memoir demonstrates the remarkable bravery and cultural competency displayed by the British. In his philosophy on governing the Sudan, Jackson said:

> What was it in the peoples of the Sudan that won the sympathy and affection of the British official? The Arabs, Nuba, Dinka . . . had nothing in common except their common humanity . . . Yet a District Commissioner despite his daily difficulties and the hostility he so frequently encountered regarded the particular tribe committed to his charge as the finest in the world, and fought unashamedly with the higher authorities for a larger share of the scanty funds available, so that he might make the lot of his tribesmen a little easier . . . Great though our differences, we realised, as we got to know the people in their villages or on their little farms, that we shared with them the universal human desire for the simple things of life: food, family affection, and a little fun and merriment.[5]

In one particularly poignant story, Jackson recalled an incident in which a Dinka chieftain decided to challenge the British authority. An official, Vere Fergusson, was called to address the situation. A new lake had appeared in a Dinka village, a happening that had deep spiritual meaning for the Dinka. The chieftain announced their god had informed him that this was a sign to raise arms against the British. Fergusson visited the lake in the middle of the uprising. In

5. Jackson, *Behind the Modern Sudan*, 180.

the midst of eight hundred armed spearmen, he ventured alone into the middle of the lake to make a sacrifice to their God in order to prove that God's will was in fact not to expel the British. The first sacrifice of a goat ended in failure, as the goat, which was supposed to drown, instead pulled Fergusson under the water. Fergusson consulted a friendly chief nearby, and tried again the same evening with more success. With a dash of good luck, it began to rain, and the Dinka took this as a sign of their God's blessing on the British, and the rebellion was peacefully averted. Had Fergusson been murdered there, or made some cultural mistake resulting in a rebellion, the response would have no doubt been a violent rebellion crushed by British machine guns with tens of thousands of casualties.[6] This kind of clever administration of Sudan led to a peaceful time for Martha's great-grandfathers Luak and Tan, a time when the country could begin to prosper and grow after having been ravished by slavery, the Turkish Ottoman Empire (1821–1885), and the Mahdists (1885–1899).

6. Ibid.

10

War and Independence

L UAK DID not know of the problems building in the outside world. He lived his life without education, something that until now would have been of no concern to him
and his ancestors. He couldn't have known that the world
was changing, and the days of isolation by the Sudd were
going to end suddenly. If the South of Sudan were going to
be able to survive in the post World War II period of colonistic independence, they would need an educated group
of citizens and leaders. In the British zeal to monetize the
South Sudanese economy, they neglected to educate any of
the people. The only education that was available was from
a few Christian missionaries. This oversight had disastrous
consequences later on for the South.

Thousands of miles away, during the life of Martha's
great-grandfather Tan, war broke out in Poland and eventually spread to England. Tan most likely knew nothing
of World War II, but it was an event that would radically
change the lives of his people.

Winston Churchill started his career fighting to liber-
ate Sudan from the Mahdist, and gained fame by his ac-
claimed and highly read book on his experiences in Sudan,

The River War. In 1933, he said the following in a revised introduction to that book:

> A generation has grown up which knows little of why we are in Egypt and the Soudan, and what our work there has been. Uninstructed and ignorant impressions colour the decisions not only of parliaments but of cabinets. It is my hope that the story which these pages contain may be some help and encouragement to those young men and women who have still confidence in the destiny of Britain in the Orient. They may learn from it how much harder it is to build up and acquire, than to squander and cast away.[1]

After World War II, the weakened British government hastily dumped their colonies, much to the disappointment of Churchill. There is some irony in the fact that Britain defeated a great genocidal evil in Germany, only to be weakened to the point to allow another to develop in Sudan.

Britain had originally planned for South Sudan to be a sovereign country. The educated elite in the North, however, wanted the southern land and its resources. They pushed the unified country through the British independence process. In a last ditch effort, the British educated a few in the South in the early 1950s but it was too little too late.[2] There was no educated elite in the South to represent themselves in Khartoum or in England. The independence process happened without a single southern Sudanese representative present. The mistake of the British was not so

1. Churchill, *River War,* xv.
2. Hutchinson, *Nuer Dilemmas,* 121.

much in the colonialism as it was in the abrupt change of power without proper oversight and representation.

The northern government wanted two things from the South. They wanted their resources (water, earth, and oil), and they wanted the people to convert to Islam. Again they found they were dealing with a stubborn people. The people of South Sudan realized that with independence from Egypt and England, the northern Muslims would oppress them. The southern Sudanese started fighting immediately when the British handed over independence to the North. One of the longest running wars of the twentieth century roared to life around the time when Martha's grandfather, Lange, was born. For centuries, cows, family, wives, children, and crops dominated life in southern Sudan. But for Lange and his children, their story would be one of misery, oppression, murder, rape, and war.

Jaafer Muhammad Nimeiri was born to a mailman in Omdurman (the Mahdi's capital) near the Nile River in 1930. Just as the British were relinquishing control of Sudan, Nimeiri was attending military school at the Sudanese Military College in 1952. During the first ten years of war, Nimeiri proved himself an effective military commander. He was then invited to attend the Army Command College in Fort Leavenworth, Kansas. In 1966, he graduated with excellent military training from an American institution.[3]

Just three years later, about when Martha's father Gatkuoch was born in 1969, Nimeiri launched a successful coup attempt to overthrow the government, ending one of the few periods of civilian rule in Sudan's history. He hoped

3. "Jaafar Nimeiri: President of Sudan 1969–1985." *The Times*, London, May 31, 2009.

to enhance Sudan's economy which suffered greatly due to the civil war.

In 1972, after nearly twenty years of civil war, Nimeiri began a harried attempt at peace. A peace council met in Addis Ababa, Ethiopia, and in only three days signed the landmark Addis Ababa Agreement.[4] The agreement ended fighting between the North and the South, and granted autonomy for the southern regions of Sudan. Many in the South opposed the agreement, with a recognition that the North was quite unlikely to follow through with the agreement in actually granting autonomy to the South. But the damage from the war to both sides had been so great that the agreement was accepted even though most knew it would not last. The North had not kept its promises in the past, and it was unlikely that this would change.

Chief Bol Malek from the Jurwir group of Dinka said the following about the Addis Ababa Agreement:

> We knew that we could not trust the Arabs with this agreement . . . some of our educated children knew this was a bad agreement, and we knew that war could always resume, but our people were exhausted by war and by death and we wanted to rest . . . Not having to run at the sound of guns or news of Arab soldiers descending on our villages was really a good thing . . . We wanted peace even at the expense of our dignity. . . . The peace was a war tactic, we needed to regroup, rearm, and resume at the right moment. Throughout the many years of calm following the agreement

4. Jok, *Sudan*, 67.

> I had never forgotten the necessity of going back
> to war when the time was right.[5]

In the 1970s and early 1980s, during the lifetime of Martha's father Gatkuoch, the South was beginning to rebuild after nearly twenty years of civil war. Lives were returning to normal, crops were being planted, and marriage dowries were returning to normal pre-war values of twenty to fifty head of cattle. It was probably a good time for Gatkuoch to grow up in southern Sudan; a much better time than his father Lange had grown up in.

As the peace continued and the South began to prosper, the North became wary of the rising power of the South, and Nimeiri felt intense pressure from Muslim radicals to institute stronger Muslim government in Sudan.[6] In September 1983, Nimeiri acquiesced and declared that Sudan would follow the Muslim law of Sharia in all regions, and that the official language of all regions would become Arabic. Sharia is a form of religious rule that results in extreme punishments for violations of the rules of the Quran. Adultery is punished by stoning, while theft is punished by amputation. Conversions to other religions, or apostasy, can be punished by death. Sudan had been ruled by Sharia in the past, during the rule of the Ottomans and the Mahdists in the 1800s; however, it had not been enforced in the South. The animistic and Christian South could clearly not live under the rule of Muslim Sharia. Executions, whippings for alcohol consumption, and amputations for theft began to

5. Ibid., 68.
6. Johnson, *Root Causes*, 56.

be publically aired on the national media channels.[7] Sharia was infamously remembered as the "September Laws." At the same time, Nimeiri's administration began to arrest, interrogate, and imprison Southerners in the government.

Around the same time, Chevron discovered oil in southern Sudan.[8] George H. W. Bush as US ambassador to the United Nations shared United States intelligence satellite photos with Khartoum to assist them in finding oil.[9] Chevron and Total Oil prospected and drilled throughout southern Sudan, estimating that there were some ten billion barrels of oil in Sudan (a number that was probably higher than reality). Nimeiri ignored the Addis Ababa Agreement, which allowed the southern autonomous region a share of any mining proceeds. A pipeline was eventually built, piping oil out of southern Sudan to a refinery in the north, allowing Khartoum complete control over revenues.

As Nimeiri prepared to declare Sharia, he realized that the few educated elite in the South had the capacity to organize a fight against the North. In 1982, students at the University of Wau became aware of the impending crisis.[10] The University at Wau was one of just a few universities in southern Sudan. The students at Wau were partly Christian Africans, and partly Muslim Arabs, as Wau was a mixed city. The rising hostilities towards Christians along with the nefarious policies of Nimeiri in attempting to subjugate the South sparked protests by the students in Wau.

---

7. Jok, *Sudan*, 76.

8. Johnson, *Root Causes*, 45.

9. Fake and Funk, *Scramble For Africa*, 31.

10. Jok, *Sudan*, 216.

Similar stories unfolded in Juba, Malakal, and other towns in southern Sudan.

A South Sudanese man named Yier Deng was attending Wau at the time. His brother, Benson Deng remembers the following story from Yier.

> I survived the 1985 slaughter of the black students in Wau. All of us at the university had been told that if we wanted to continue our education we must convert to be Muslims. Many students paraded in the city to speak for their rights as Sudanese, but special police forces intervened. The Arab students were separated from us and taken to their dorms. The black students were arrested and charged with causing turmoil and disobeying the Islamic laws. Some were lined up, made to kneel by the riverbank and executed. Their heads were cut off with a machete and thrown in the river. We were led to the dorms and questioned. "Do you know the leader of the rebels, John Garang?" "Do you want to join them?" The students who resisted with loud voices were tied together, sprinkled with paraffin, and burned alive. They locked the rest of us in the dorm. I was with many friends that I haven't seen again. We heard noises outside and saw they were preparing to burn down the whole dorm. We broke a window and ran, but a squad of troops was guarding the building. They fired; only three of us made it to the woods, leaving behind our moaning injured friends.[11]

11. B. Deng et al., *They Poured Fire on Us*, 164.

PART II: THE LONG ROOTS OF WAR

Civil war roared to life once again. If Nimeiri had any hopes for peace and equality in the South, they were now lost. Nimeiri's administration went on to conduct war, targeting civilians in southern Sudan with unprecedented brutality.

11

The Second War

JOHN GARANG was born in Bor County along the White Nile. He was born to the Dinka clan of southern Sudan to a poor family, and his parents died while he was young. A relative sent him to boarding school in Wau, but he was forced to attend secondary school in Tanzania due to the violence in Sudan. He was fortunate enough to win a scholarship to study abroad in the United States, and earned a degree from a small liberal arts college in Iowa, Grinnell University. Then, in the 1970s he earned a PhD in agriculture from Iowa State University. By the 1980s he was a rising star in the peacetime unified Sudanese military, which had unified under the Addis Ababa Agreement. After the September Laws were initiated by Nimeiri, Garang headed south from his headquarters in Omdurman to join his fellow Southerners. He was one of the very few educated leaders available in the South, and it was immediately realized that he could fulfill the need for strong leadership. He defected from the northern controlled military and quickly built up a small force of rebels. He organized a new political and military rebel group called the Sudanese People Liberation Army and Movement (SPLA/SPLM). Yier Deng and tens of thousands of other southern Sudanese men and boys joined the fight in an effort to gain autonomy for their people under the leadership of Garang and the SPLA. The SPLA was, and still is, the key unifying organization in the South.

John Garang and the SPLA were left with no choice except to fight the north. However, the consequences of their decision to fight were catastrophic for their people, particularly for the children.

During this time of war, amid great suffering, a group of twenty thousand mostly orphaned southern Sudanese boys wandered a thousand miles across Sudan. These "Lost Boys" were civilian children separated from their families during the war, mostly during attacks on civilians by the Nimeiri regime. The boys wandered into refugee camps in Ethiopia and Kenya trying to escape the violence. There were also a few "Lost girls" at this time, but the majority were boys. Nearly half of them died from starvation, lion attacks, and enemy attacks while on their journey. The Lost Boys have garnered significant press attention in the West, but sadly, Martha would suffer the same fate some twenty years later.

The following excerpts are very graphic depictions of violent acts that occurred during this time. Sensitive readers may want to skip the following three quotations.

One of the lost boys, Benson Deng, remembers hearing a northern leader saying the following during a radio address.

> The abeed [slave] stinks and goes naked! Dinka are the disobedient rebel tribe and criminal to the Arabs. Go! Go! Go to the south and find him grass and bush rotting with hunber. Crush the

Dinkas! Let them run for days and nights. Next year, all of the Sudan will be smelly with the Dinka children born and rotting in jailhouses. Bring the Dinkas to jail. If they disobey, the barrels of tanks and Antonov can escort them here.[1]

Benson remembers an incident where the Murahiliin gunmen attacked:

Horsemen attacked and killed countless villagers at Warawar, just north of our village. They burned the crops and nailed a baby on a fig tree like Jesus on the cross. People who knew how to read said the dot marks on the paper said, "Jesus, your God was here."[2]

Another lost boy, Alephonsion Deng, remembers one poignant atrocity from his home village in southern Sudan. Alepho, who was about six years old at the time, remembers playing with a little girl who had a deformity that made walking difficult. Alepho's sister, Angong explained the cause of the little girl's deformity.

You are nearly a man and this is a time of war, you should understand these things that happen. The men had guns. One of them wanted to take the little girl with him but she clung to a small bush screaming in terror so it was difficult for him to remove her hands. "You little stupid girl," the man shouted. "I will give you the medicine you will never forget." He stooped over her and pulled out his penis. We screamed but there was nothing her mother or I could do. They had

1. B. Deng et al., *They Poured Fire on Us*, 189.
2. Ibid., 164.

us tied lying on our stomachs and held us back
with guns. The man tried to dig his penis into
the girl, but he couldn't get it in while he was
holding her down too. He got up and tied her
hands to that small bush. He pushed it in and
pushed and pushed on her with his full weight.
At first she struggled and screamed, but a few
minutes later the loud cries stopped. The little
girl had passed out. I couldn't look at this act
one more minute. To my disgrace all I did was
lie on my belly and cry. The man raised his gun
to shoot the girl in her head, but another man
argued with him. They didn't shoot her and left.[3]

These wretched acts are inexcusable for any cause,
but it's particularly terrible that they were done in the
name of Islam. The Northerners rationalized that these
evil acts were acceptable if practiced on infidels, saying the
non-Muslim inhabitants of southern Sudan were not truly
human. However, later this rationalization failed when
Northerners attacked, raped, and killed black Muslims in
Darfur.

During the cold war, the United States provided a
significant amount of support to Nimeiri throughout the
1980s without regard to the human rights atrocities taking
place. Economic support to Sudan was greater than that
to any country in Sub-Saharan Africa, with $160 million
yearly in economic support and $100 million yearly in
military support.[4] The military support was purportedly
to prevent the spread of communism from players such

3. Ibid., 97.
4. Johnson, *Root Causes*, 43.

as Libya. In fact, the money was used directly against the South. The US government saw Garang and the SPLA as a socialist organization and hence closer to communism, ignoring the fact that Nimeiri was a brutal military dictator who was initially communist.[5]

From the earliest days of independence from Britain, the Khartoum government intended for Sudan to be united under Islam, using military force if necessary. Sadiq Al-Mahdi, Prime Minister of Sudan in 1968 (and again in 1986), had gone on record in international travel saying that the quickest path to Sudanese unity was to make the South Muslim. It was said that he even pleaded with the Pope, "To agree with him to convert all Southern Sudanese into 'believers,' whether Muslim or Christian."[6] However, there is no question that the goal was complete submission to Islam, even if it required some level of genocide to remove the Christians from the South. The government's brutal methods, however, had the opposite effect. Instead of capitulating to forced conversions, the people of South Sudan were flocking to Christianity. When the government expelled Christian missionaries in 1964, Christianity began to explode.[7] After Nimeiri instituted the September Laws, the Catholic Church in Wau swelled to the point that mass could no longer be conducted indoors; it had to be conducted in the open air to facilitate the crowds.[8] Lual Diing Wol, an SPLA commander, said the following in 2003:

5. Jok, *Sudan*, 50.

6. Johnson, *Root Causes*, 35, and Jok, *Sudan*, 64.

7. Johnson, *Root Causes*, 35.

8. Jok, *Sudan*, 78.

> In the past, our people never used to talk about being African or Christian or non-Arab because they did not need to prove to anyone what their identity was. People professing Christianity used to go to church when they felt like it and not because they wanted to demonstrate their Christian commitments to anyone. But since 1983, it has become a question of showing the government and its Muslim zealots that we are proud of our identity and do not want anybody to change us. This insistence of Northern rulers that our country must become Arab or Muslim has only created a sense of extremism to prove the opposite . . . I cannot see how all of its regions will remain together in a united country if one group feels that their identity should become the identity of the entire nation.[9]

In 1986, Nimeiri was ousted, and Sadiq al-Mahdi returned to power. For three years, Sudan operated under civilian rule, without cessation of the civil war. In 1989, any hope of peace was doused by a bloodless military coup lead by Omar al-Bashir.

Unlike Nimeiri, Al Bashir was raised and trained completely in Sudan and the Middle East. Al Bashir expanded and encouraged Muslim rule in Sudan along with Sharia. The "southern problem" had been a point of significant debate in northern Sudan, given that the war had a massively negative impact on the economy and culture in Sudan. Al Bashir came from the point of view that the only way to address the "southern problem" was with the military.

9. Jok, *Sudan*, 78.

In the early 1990s Khartoum began to exploit a division within the SPLA. Old tribal conflicts were beginning to take hold within a Nuer-Dinka split of the SPLA. Bashir saw this as an opportunity to splinter the SPLA and provide an upper hand to the North in the battle. Bashir funded the splinter group, referred to as the Nasir faction, and encouraged the image of the main SPLA branch as a Dinka led organization under the Dinka leadership of John Garang. The war became a three-way war, between the Dinka, Nuer, and the North. Chaos reigned. It was unclear who the enemy was. Al Bashir also funded the deeply evil northern Ugandan rebel group, the Lord's Resistance Army (LRA).[10] The LRA began raiding the southernmost parts of southern Sudan. The consequences for civilians in the South were devastating. These same practices were used effectively (although on a smaller scale) in the more recent Darfurian conflict where Al-Bashir funded the Janjaweed against the Darfurians.[11]

This is not to say that the North solely committed the atrocities. As the war wore on, the SPLA became desperate for food and supplies, and often forcefully took them from civilians. As the SPLA splintered into tribal warfare, attacks by both sides on civilian populations increased. The North then blamed the southern problem on intertribal fighting in order to wash their hands of guilt. In all cases the families in the villages paid the price. Some of the more egregious acts by the SPLA involved recruiting child soldiers. Decades of war had depleted the SPLA of its soldiers. Eventually, the SPLA drew from the pool of young

10. Johnson, *Root Causes*, 100.

11. Fake and Funk, *Scramble for Africa*, 22.

81

teenagers to fill their ranks. No doubt there were voluntary recruits from the many internally displaced kids without families, but often that was not the case. They captured children and held them in camps lacking food and water until they reached a fighting age. Sadly, this has left deep scars on the youth, and now the men, of southern Sudan.[12]

To address the deep financial woes of the country, largely caused by the protracted civil war, Al Bashir aggressively courted oil companies. Sudan has about five billion barrels of proven oil reserves. To any benevolent leader, this represents hundreds of billions of dollars of development funds that could easily educate every child in Sudan while building roads, hospitals, and buildings necessary to spur economic development. Instead, Al Bashir used the money to fund the Khartoum military effort. Oil money became the means to crush the resistance in the South and fund the upcoming war in Darfur.[13]

Chevron was involved in the initial oil explorations but held the oil in reserve waiting for better pricing. Partly due to the war, it never brought Sudan's oil into significant production. The United States took a strong stance against the human rights violations in Sudan after Nimeiri's overthrow, and restricted US economic involvement in the northern regime. The Canadians and Swedes, however, did not have such legislation. The Canadian oil company Talisman developed the oil fields, investing heavily on behalf of Bashir's regime. Talisman built airfields in the South to support oil operations, which the northern government

12. Jal, *War Child*, 65–85.

13. Gagnon and Ryle, "Investigation into Oil Development," 2.

used directly to attack nearby civilian populations.[14] SPLA rebel groups targeted oil operations to try to limit the northern government's funding source. Eventually, Talisman was sued by the Presbyterian Church in American courts (since they were listed on the New York Stock Exchange), under grounds that the company was supporting human rights violations.[15] American church groups were pivotal in convincing the American and Canadian governments to take the human rights violations in Sudan seriously. Talisman was admonished and eventually they divested their share to an Indian oil company called ONGC Videsh. China and India then became the major funders of the oil industry in Sudan. China in particular turned a blind eye against Sudan's human rights violations.

By the late 1990s, the oil money was flowing into Sudan. Khartoum purchased weapons, gunships, and ammunition from the Soviets and Chinese as the cold war wound down. These weapons were largely used to attack civilian populations in the South.

Jok Madut Jok recalls the following story of the weapons funded by the oil money.

> A UN World Food Program staff member who was in charge of food distribution described the attack: "The gunship maintained its position right over the WFP compound and started shooting sideways aiming at the huts across the compound. Missiles/rockets were used to blow up hut after hut with large numbers of people

14. Ibid.

15. Presbyterian Church of Sudan et al. v. Talisman Energy, Inc. 07–0016, United States Court of Appeals (2d Cir. 2009).

> inside, followed by machine guns aimed at those running for cover." Those who were in the huts were either children, sick people, or elderly, the more vulnerable who were waiting for their mothers or sisters to return with food from WFP distribution.[16]

Throughout the late 1990s, the United States was staunchly against the Khartoum government's human rights violations. In 1997, the Clinton administration imposed broad sanctions against Sudan. Although the sanctions were damaging to Sudan, one of their most important exports was exempted from the sanctions. Gum arabic is a tar made from Acacia Senegal trees. It is used as an emulsifier in a surprisingly large number of products ranging from newspapers and pharmaceuticals to soft drinks. Sudan is the largest world supplier of gum arabic, and the soft drink industry heavily lobbied to exempt it from the sanctions. Both the Clinton and Bush administrations caved to the soft drink companies, keeping the profitable government-owned gum arabic growers in business. In 2007, the Sudanese ambassador to the United States threatened to halt gum arabic shipments if the United States continued to pressure Sudan on the Darfurian conflict,[17] playing on the soda industry's supply chain fears. It is a great irony that severe human rights violations are trumped by Americans' thirst for soda.

Martha's village was attacked around 2002. For a considerable amount of time, the remoteness of Martha's

16. Jok, *Sudan*, 177.

17. Dana Milbank, "Denying Genocide in Darfur—and Americans Their Coca-Cola." *Washington Post*, May 31, 2007.

village protected her and her family. But the oil money intensified the war, and eventually the holocaust found her. It found her first through airplanes bought from Russia to bomb her village, and later by foot soldiers carrying weapons funded by oil money. The holocaust was in full swing, as southern Sudan became a killing field of black Africans.

The September 11, 2001, attacks provided a strategic opportunity for Bashir to gain support from the West. He wisely played on the terrorism fears to insulate his government from human rights criticism. Osama Bin Laden had lived in Sudan during the 1990s and worked with Bashir's government.[18] Bashir offered intelligence information on Osama and in return got the support and blessing of Bush's administration.[19]

Christian groups in America, however, kept up the pressure on the administration to condemn Sudan. This pressure was largely effective, and the state department began to broker a peace deal between the Khartoum government and the SPLA. In 2005, the two parties signed the Comprehensive Peace Agreement, ending the fifty-year civil war. John Garang was made the Vice President of Sudan, and the South was given a certain amount of autonomy. Three weeks later, Garang was killed in a mysterious helicopter crash. Both the Sudanese government and the SPLA blamed bad weather, but the timing of his death inevitably raised questions about the circumstances of the crash.

The Comprehensive Peace Agreement stipulated that a referendum be held in January 2011 to decide the fate of

18. Jok, *Sudan*, 136.
19. Ibid., 255.

southern Sudan. The agreement held that the people would be able to vote on whether or not they wanted an independent state in the South. On January 9, 2011, the southern Sudanese people overwhelmingly voted for independence in what might be the most one-sided national referendum in the history of democracy. Of the 3.8 million southern Sudanese voters, 98.9 percent voted for succession, leaving less than 50,000 residents voting for Sudanese unity.

Many believe that the referendum could catalyze the third civil war in Sudan, as the two parties will fight over oil and the newly formed borders. The intertribal fighting instigated by Bashir will continue to haunt the South for decades to come. Fifty years of war crimes in the South will undoubtedly be hard to address. The culture of guns has become deeply embedded within tribal culture in Sudan. Instead of cattle dowries, fathers now bestow guns upon their son-in-law's family.[20] Instead of traditional tribal markings cut into teenage boys becoming men, depictions of assault rifles are embedded in their skin.[21]

But there is hope. Martha and I attended one of the many South Sudanese independence celebrations on July 9, 2011, in San Jose, California. No doubt, the difficulties of war were not far away for the group of Sudanese refugees assembled there. But against all odds, everyone believed that southern Sudan would find peace and prosperity. Almost every Sudanese person in attendance planned to eventually return to their homeland to contribute to their new country. It is Martha's generation that will decide the

20. Hutchinson, *Nuer Dilemmas*, 156.
21. Peraino, "Sorry, Sudan," 40.

future of Sudan. If Martha is any indication, the future is very bright indeed!

12

Twenty-First-Century Genocide

IN 2004, the world stopped to remember the genocide in Rwanda, where eight hundred thousand people were slaughtered with machetes for reasons that made little sense to anyone. The world stopped to say, "Never again." At the same time, after intense debate, the US government officially declared that genocide was happening in South Sudan and in Darfur (in western Sudan). So much for "Never again."

On November 11, 1917, at 11:11 p.m., the world stopped to celebrate the end of the Great War. Everyone agreed that it was to be the final world war, and a number of measures were put into place to assure that the agreement would stand. The war reparations against Germany would prevent it from militarizing again. The Nations League would help to prevent war by providing a world forum to solve problems.

As we all know, the peace was short lived. In less than twenty years, the German war machine defeated most of Europe. Adolf Hitler oversaw the attempted elimination of the Jews, Gypsies, gays, elderly, and others. Six million were slaughtered in stunningly efficient German engineered death machines.

I have visited a German concentration camp in Dachau. The theme is clear: "Never again." The Germans take this very seriously.

Sadly, the twentieth century has been a long string of "never agains." So far in the southern Sudan genocide, 2.5 million people have been killed and millions more have been displaced.[1] Many hundreds of thousands more have been killed in Darfur.

There is debate about whether or not genocide has actually occurred in southern Sudan or in Darfur. In July 2010, the International Criminal Court issued an arrest warrant for Al-Bashir, accusing him of genocide, war crimes, and crimes against humanity committed in Darfur. An earlier United Nations commission had determined that genocide had not occurred, as specified by the technical definition of genocide from the 1948 Genocide Convention rulings.

At some point, the debate about the word "genocide" is academic. Whether or not genocide happened by the technical definition, there is no doubt that heinous war crimes against humanity were committed over a course of fifty years by the Khartoum government. The focus should not be on the terminology, it should be on the war crimes, the repercussions on the people, and the healing process.

---

1. The death toll is widely cited at 2.5 million, but the truth is that no one knows what it actually is. At some points, cited death tolls have even exceeded the total population of the southern region. It is certain, however, that a very significant percentage of the population was killed or displaced. For more commentary, see Johnson, *Root Causes*, 143.

13

Cost of Technology

THE WEST offered civilization to southern Sudan. But it seems that Sudan received more damage than profit from the bargain. Moorehead offered this perspective and the situation at the turn of the twentieth century. Sadly, the circumstances have only grown worse since then.

> The population of the Sudan had dwindled to a bare two million . . . In some areas rinderpest had entirely wiped out the herds of domestic cattle and even worse plagues were soon to follow. For many hundreds of miles the banks of the White Nile were a desolation. In the light of this one was permitted to wonder whether the price paid for civilization was not too high. "The Nile-land of today . . . ," Harry Johnston wrote at the turn of the century, "is much of it in sad contrast with its condition during [the 1800s] . . . It is sad to think that the people were possibly happier [then]."[1]

The technological advancements that our society has pushed forward in the past few hundred years have been truly amazing. My great-grandmother died when she was one hundred and eight years old. She remembers the first

1. Moorehead, *White Nile*, 384.

time she used a phone, the first time she heard a radio, the first car, the first airplane, and the first computer. In her hundred-year lifetime, more technological progress was made than in the history of the world combined. It can be argued that this progress has been great for us, as long as you define "us" as people in the West. We've generated tremendous wealth, solved famine and hunger, cured most diseases, and created a much less laborious lifestyle.

But if you define "us" as a third world country, particularly in Sudan, the impact of technology has not been so rosy. Wealth has not been generated; division between the wealthy nations and poor nations has only grown larger. Hunger has not improved, and in some cases has gotten worse due to political problems and regional climate changes. War and weapons have created disastrous results. Many African countries have actually had decreased life expectancies due to war and AIDS.[2] Indeed, Africa has experienced many disadvantages of technology, but has enjoyed few of the benefits.

It's impossible to discuss the recent history of Sudan without considering the negative impact of technology. War and murder are as old as humans in southern Sudan. However, before the introduction of modern weapons, there was a system of checks and balances in place that had developed during the centuries of isolation provided by the Sudd. Most fighting was done with spears. Each spear had markings that could be identified by its owner who was required by tradition to identify himself as the killer. Deaths from war or family clashes had to be compensated with an

2. "Human Development Report 2002," 176.

exchange of cattle.[3] The cattle cost of murder could be more than dowry costs, which would be disastrous for a family since it could prevent a son from marrying due to lack of dowry. This provided a system of balance in a society without jails or police.

The introduction of guns changed this equation fundamentally. During gun battles flying bullets can't be traced back to a source. Murder can't be proven, and perpetrators can't be identified.[4] In the West, we've solved this problem by using modern forensics which can, in fact, trace a bullet back to a gun by its unique microscopic markings. But of course that technology is not available in Sudan. This and a plethora of other problems related to the negative consequences of technology haunt southern Sudan.

It goes without saying that the genocide of southern Sudan would be impossible without modern weaponry. The same was true for Nazi Germany; however, Germany was able to access technology and wealth after the war through the Marshal Plan in order to recover. South Sudan has a steady income stream through its considerable oil revenues; however, lack of transportation infrastructure, ethnic violence, and lack of education will make closing the technology gap very difficult.

The unending gerbil wheel of technological innovation needs to change. What if we spent less time putting videos on our cell phones, and instead focused our energy on addressing the fundamental problems that plague our world? Imagine what would happen if the full power of our

3. Hutchinson, *Nuer Dilemmas*, 156.
4. Ibid.

economic and technological machine were reoriented to helping the poor instead of enriching the rich?

If the twentieth century was the century of tech-nological innovation for the wealthy, my hope is that the twenty-first century will be the century of responsibly disseminating that technology throughout the world to help both the poor and the rich. I hope that the next great breakthrough won't be a new computer or cell phone, but instead a cure for malaria, or a disease – resistant corn crop for equatorial Africa, or a new financial system that encour-ages productive commerce in Africa instead of oppression.

There is debate about whether large-scale governmen-tal aid to nations such as Sudan is helpful or damaging to the long-term prospects of the country. Throughout the early 1980s, the UN forbade aid distribution to SPLA-controlled areas in South Sudan at the urging of the United States since the SPLA was seen as a communist organization. What food was scheduled for delivery to the South was often diverted to feed the northern army. After severe flooding and famine in 1988, which received extensive press coverage, Operation Lifeline Sudan (OLS) was started by UNICEF to supply food aid to southern Sudan in SPLA-controlled territory. However, Khartoum still had overall control of distribu-tion plans, and required that food aid only be distributed to the Nassir faction that the North was supporting against the main branch of the SPLA.[5] The Sudanese government has used aid as a tool in its war with the South, diverting food aid to its own soldiers, or using food aid to herd large numbers of people into so-called "peace camps" for future

5. Johnson, *Root Causes*, 148.

attacks.[6] Furthermore, the ongoing aid has become a crutch used by the Khartoum government to ignore the needs of its own people and instead pour its investment moneys into wartime weapons.

It has been clearly demonstrated that long-term food aid hurts local economies by undercutting agriculture.[7] It has been similarly shown that free clothing distributed by aid agencies cripples local textiles initiatives.[8] This is particularly troublesome since countries have traditionally industrialized on precisely those two industries: textiles and agriculture. The huge influx of foreign aid into Sudan can have unintended consequences. *Newsweek* reports that recent rent for western style houses in Juba, the capital of southern Sudan, can exceed $12,000 per month due to high demand and lack of availability.[9] This kind of radical influx can have destabilizing effects in a region that has historically been so poor, as it pulls talented workers away from sustainable industries into aid complexes that will one day evaporate.

The good news is that in the past few decades a great deal has been learned about successful foreign aid and development programs. It has been learned that food aid should only be used as a bridge through times of famine or disaster, after which it is replaced with agricultural assistance. Free clothing is replaced by micro loans to help local economies develop their own textile industry. Education

6. Jok, *Sudan*, 18.

7. Murphy and McAfee, "U. S. Food Aid," and Johnson, *Root Causes*, 144.

8. Frazer, "Used-Clothing Donations."

9. Peraino, "Sorry, Sudan," 38.

for girls has been shown to be particularly important in developing countries. Educated girls turn into educated mothers, which tend to turn into educated households. The effect of educating a young girl can ripple throughout the community as she grows and starts to have children, having a tremendous effect.[10] Our aid efforts should be focused on these best practices: agricultural development assistance, micro loans, and solid education for both boys and girls. The good news is that none of these are high-cost items; none requires large-scale infrastructure investments. They require only basic security for aid workers, small investments in building schools, and modest ongoing investments in paying and training local teachers.

Fortunately, there are many small-scale organizations operating in southern Sudan that are doing exactly the right things. One such organization is Mercy Beyond Borders, run by Sister Marilyn Lacey.[11] It is incredible what small-scale organizations like Mercy Beyond Borders can accomplish with limited funds. Sister Marilyn reports that in 2010 on a budget of only a few hundred thousand dollars, they were able to send more girls to the national high school qualifying exam in Kenya than any other school in the region. They have many girls attending high school on scholarships, which cost about two thousand dollars for four years of school. The cost of high school education per student in Sudan is nearly ten times less than that of a high school education in the United States, making this a very high dividend investment, especially given the ripple effect

10. Hillman and Jenkner, *Educating Children in Poor Countries*.

11. Learn more about this organization by visiting their web site: http://www.mercybeyondborders.org/.

of educating a girl in a poor community. They have literacy programs for women, micro-loan programs for women with HIV/AIDs, nursing and health education programs, and a variety of other community building programs. The atrocities committed against millions of southern Sudanese just like Martha are hard to comprehend. But we are not powerless to help the healing process in southern Sudan. Mercy Beyond Borders is doing the real work of educating and healing a people that have been brutally oppressed. If you have been touched by Martha's story, please consider partnering with Mercy Beyond Borders to help alleviate the suffering of thousands of women who were not as fortunate as Martha to have immigrated to America.

14

Peace

RECENTLY I walked the Stations of the Cross at Our Lady of Peace in Santa Clara, California. Since the fifteenth century, Franciscan Christians have built sets of fourteen outdoor stations depicting the journey of Christ from his accusation to his death and burial. These have become an iconic way of reliving the suffering and experience of Jesus in his final days.

In the past, when I've walked the stations I've been struck by the suffering of Christ in the latter depictions. But on this day, I stopped at the first stations. There was Jesus, bound and on trial in front of Pontius Pilate. He was falsely accused and tried for a crime that did not exist; even Pontius Pilate knew he was innocent. Nonetheless, he was found guilty and sentenced to capital punishment. That was so deeply unfair, yet Jesus in his wisdom did not complain or fight. He simply said, "My kingdom is not of this world. If it were, my servants would fight to prevent my arrest by the Jews. But now my kingdom is from another place . . . In fact, for this reason I was born, and for this I came into the world, to testify to the truth. Everyone on the side of truth listens to me" (John 18:36–37 NIV).

Even in the deepest moment of Jesus's suffering, he was at peace. He had no need to defend himself against unjust charges.

I am not like that. When I've been wronged, I want to fight it. I am indignant. Mistreatments loom heavy in my heart. I often do not have peace.

But Jesus was not this way. He had peace. No doubt he suffered and fully felt the pain; however, he had peace. His peace allowed him to accept his suffering without indignation, without fighting it. His suffering did not break him. Conversely, he saved the world by suffering.

I have given many things to Martha of value in the world: time, money, knowledge, and help navigating a difficult world.

But she has given me a gift that is far greater than anything I have to give her.

As you read the pages of her story, you experienced the depth of her suffering. She has reason to be angry, bitter, and broken. However, she is none of those things. She has peace. Everyone who knows Martha can sense her peace. It is displayed by her quiet confidence when others misbehave or look for shortcuts. She is at peace; she can withstand the pressure to do wrong. Her peace radiates all around her, enveloping the lives surrounding her. As she holds my new infant in her arms, I can see her peace and calmness fill the room. It flows from her like the ceaselessness of the Nile.

Most people who know Martha have no idea what incredible suffering lies behind her peace. I did not know myself until her words came spilling out into this book. Now I know.

I have found the gift that Jesus has brought into my home and family. His suffering lives here. And so does his peace. Martha, I have much to learn from you. May I find your peace in my small sufferings and may Jesus meet us both there. May the good people of southern Sudan share the same peace as they build their new nation. May hope and love obliterate the evil of war that has so long plagued Sudan. May peace reign for us all!

Martha's Ancestors

Ancestor	Year	Events in Sudan
	540	Kingdoms of Nubia, Muqurra, and Alwa form
	1205	Theodora sends first missionaries to Nubia
	1500	Nubians send armies to help Coptic Christians in Egypt
	1500	Muslims start to overtake Christians in northern Sudan
	1504	Funj kingdom formed in Nubia, takes over Alwa
	1700s	Decline of Funj
Kakere (Half Bowl)	1770	
Keer (Lake)	1790	
Jiohk (Dog)	1810	
	1821	Muhammad Ali of Ottamans defeats Funj, Sharia is enforced
Quane (Bowl)	1830	
Jal (Walk)	1850	
	1860	Egypt outlaws slave raiding due to European pressure, but does not enforce policy
Kucck (Thorn)	1870	

Martha's Ancestors

Ancestor	Year	Events in Sudan
	1874	Charles Gordon given the task of ending slavery in Sudan
	1884–1898	Mahdists govern Sudan
	1885	Gordon killed by Mahdists
Gong (Fish Hook)	1892	British Commander Herbert Kitchener begins another conquest of Sudan
	1896	Twenty-five thousand British and Egyptian troops attack Mahdists
	1899	Anglo-Egyptian Condominium forms, England and Egypt begin rule of Sudan
Luak (Barn)	1910	
	1922	Egypt gains independence, England takes over governance of Sudan
Tang (Spear Shaft)	1930	England allows indirect indigenous rule of Sudan
	1920s and 1930s	Christian missionaries make converts in South Sudan and begin education programs
	1942	Sudan begins to move towards independence
	1940–1945	WWII
Lange (Mosquito Net)	1950	
	1952	Sudan negotiates for independence without representation from the South; British officers warn that a united Sudan will result in civil war, but warnings go unheeded
	1955	Civil war begins with mutiny when Southern Soldiers are transferred to Northern control

Ancestor	Year	Events in Sudan
	1955	Formation of the southern rebel group Anyanya (meaning snake venom)
	1956	Sudan achieves united independence
	1958–1964	Abbud military government escalates civil war
	1964–1969	Civilian rule under Sadiq Al Mahdi
	1969	Military coup, Nimeiri begins rule
Gatkuoch (Son of God)	1971	Joseph Lagu starts Southern Sudan Liberation Movement (SSLM)
	1972	Addis Ababa Agreement ends first civil war
	Sept 1983	Nimeiri declares Sharia, known as "September Laws"
	1983	Civil war erupts again
	1986–1989	Civilian rule under Sadiq Al-Mahdi, war continues
	1989	Omar Al Bashir leads military coup, takes control of government
Martha	1992	
Koat Daniel	1995	
Matthew	1996	
Paul Rout	1999	
	2002	Martha's village attacked, family flees to Uganda
	2007	Family immigrates to America

Bibliography

Churchill, Winston S. The River War. London: Prion, 1962.

Deng, Benson, Alephonsion Benson, and Ajak Benjamin. They Poured Fire on Us from the Sky: The True Story of Three Lost Boys from Sudan. New York: PublicAffairs, 2005.

Deng, Francis Mading. Africans of Two Worlds: The Dinka in Afro-Arab Sudan. London: Yale University Press, 1978.

Fake, Steven, and Kevin Funk. The Scramble for Africa. Montreal: Black Rose Books, 2009.

Frazer, Garth. "Used-Clothing Donations and Apparel Production in Africa." Economic Journal 118, no. 532 (2008) 1764–84.

Gagnon, Georgette, and John Ryle. Report of an Investigation into Oil Development, Conflict and Displacement in Western Upper Nile. Funded by Canadian and British non-governmental organzations, October 2001.

Hillman, Arye, and Eva Jenkner. Educating Children in Poor Countries. Economic Issues, vol. 33. Washington, DC: International Monetary Fund, 2004.

Hutchinson, Sharon E. Nuer Dilemmas: Coping with Money, War, and the State. Berkeley, CA: University of California Press, 1996.

Jackson, Henry Cecil. Behind the Modern Sudan. New York: St. Martin's Press, 1955.

Jal, Emmanuel. War Child: A Child Soldier's Story. New York: St. Martin's Press, 2009.

Johnson, Douglas Hamilton. The Root Causes of Sudan's Civil Wars. Bloomington: Indiana University Press, 1994.

Jok, Madut Jok. Sudan: Race Religion and Violence. Oxford, England: Oneworld Publications, 2007.

Metz, Helen Chapin. Sudan: A Country Study. Washington, D.C.: Headquarters Dept. of Army, 1992.

Bibliography

Moorehead, Alan. The White Nile. New York: Harper and Row, 2000.

Murphy, Sophia, and Kathy McAfee. "U. S. Food Aid: Time to Get It Right." Minneapolis: Institute for Agriculture and Trade Policy, 2005.

Peraino, Kevin. "Sorry, Sudan." Newsweek 156, no. 14 (October 4, 2010) 36–41.

Presbyterian Church of Sudan et al. v. Talisman Energy, Inc. 07–0016, New York: United States Court of Appeals (2d Cir. 2009).

Shorter, Aylward. "Lourdel Siméon, 1853–1890, Catholic, Uganda." In Dictionary of African Christian Biography. No Pages. Online: http://www.dacb.org/stories/uganda/lourdel_simeon.html.

Speke, John Hanning. Journal of the Discovery of the Source of the Nile. London: William Blackwood and Sons, 1863.

Uganda Martyrs Shrine. No Pages. Online: http://www.ugandamartyrsshrine.org.ug/details.php?id=8.

United Nations Development Programme. "Human Development Report 2002." New York: Oxford University Press, 2002.